Physical Characteristics of the

(from rd)

Body: Firm. Back strong, straight and broad. Brisket deep and long; moderate tuck up.

Tail: Medium length, covered with long hair. Carried curved over the back when dog is moving.

Coat: Profuse. Outer coat long and coarse. Undercoat soft and thick. Shorter on the head and front parts of legs.

Colour: All colours are allowed, but the main colour must dominate. Marks differing from the dominant colour are permitted on head, neck, chest, legs and on tip of tail.

Size: Height: dogs 46–52 cms (18–20.5 ins) at withers; bitches: 41–47 cms (16–18.5 ins) at withers.

Hindquarters: Strong boned. Strong and straight when viewed from behind. Hock of medium size. Dewclaws permitted.

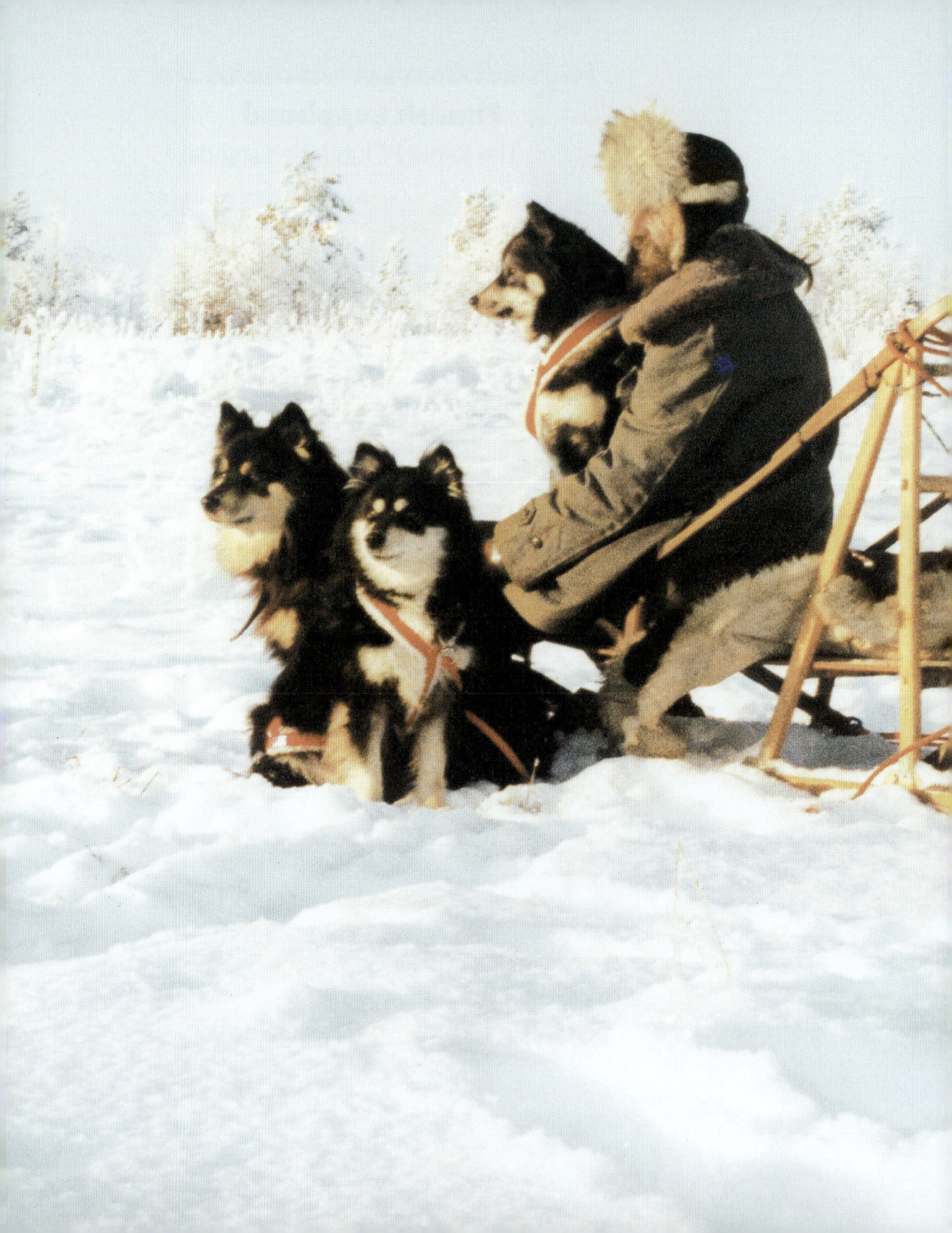

Finnish Lapphund

By Toni Jackson

9   History of the Finnish Lapphund

Meet the reindeer herders of Lapland, a land of rugged terrain and extreme winters. Follow the development of these dogs, their separation into distinct breeds and the establishment of the Finnish Lapphund. Acquaint yourself with instrumental breeders, the formation of breed clubs and the Lapphund's spread to countries beyond its homeland.

32   Characteristics of the Finnish Lapphund

Hardy and versatile, the Finnish Lapphund is an able herder, faithful companion and skilled participant in many activities and areas of the dog sport. Learn about the breed in looks, temperament and aptitudes to decide if you're ready to add a Finnish friend to the family.

56   Breed Standard for the Finnish Lapphund

Learn the requirements of a well-bred Finnish Lapphund by studying the description of the breed as set forth in the Fédération Cynologique Internationale's breed standard. Both show dogs and pets must possess key characteristics as outlined in the breed standard.

63   Your Puppy Finnish Lapphund

Be advised about choosing a reputable breeder and selecting a healthy, typical puppy. Understand the responsibilities of ownership, including home preparation, acclimatisation, the vet and prevention of common puppy problems.

86   Everyday Care of Your Finnish Lapphund

Enter into a sensible discussion of dietary and feeding considerations, exercise, grooming, travelling and identification of your dog. This chapter discusses Finnish Lapphund care for all stages of development.

Contents

Training Your Finnish Lapphund — 100

By Charlotte Schwartz
Be informed about the importance of training your Finnish Lapphund from the basics of toilet training and understanding the development of a young dog to executing obedience commands (sit, stay, down, etc.).

Health Care of Your Finnish Lapphund — 127

Discover how to select a qualified vet and care for your dog at all stages of life. Topics include vaccinations, skin problems, dealing with external and internal parasites and common medical and behavioural conditions.

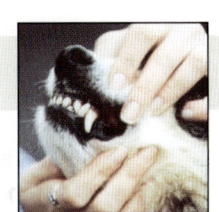

Index 156

KENNEL CLUB BOOKS: FINNISH LAPPHUND
ISBN: 1-59378-374-4

Copyright © 2003 Kennel Club Books, Inc.
308 Main Street, Allenhurst, NJ 07711 USA
Cover Design Patented: US 6,435,559 B2 • Printed in South Korea

All rights reserved. No part of this book may be reproduced in any form, by photostat, scanner, microfilm, xerography or any other means, or incorporated into any information retrieval system, electronic or mechanical, without the written permission of the copyright owner.

Photography by Carol Ann Johnson, with additional photographs by:

Erwin and Peggy Bauer, Norvia Behling, TJ Calhoun, Carolina Biological Supply, Juliette Cunliffe, Doskocil, Mrs S M Dunger, Isabelle Francais, James Hayden-Yoav, James R Hayden, RBP, Toni Jackson, Bill Jonas, Dwight R Kuhn, Dr Dennis Kunkel, Mikki Pet Products, Marika Niemelä, Petra Palukka, Phototake, Jean Claude Revy, Dr Andrew Spielman, Terhi Uski and Alice van Kempen.

Illustrations by Patricia Peters.

The publisher wishes to thank all of the owners of the dogs featured in this book, including Toni Jackson, Anelle Lundgen, Liz Mowatt and Rauno Nisula.

8 FINNISH LAPPHUND

Author Toni Jackson winning Best in Match with a nine-year-old Finnish Lapphund under judge Juliette Cunliffe during a Rare Breed Match. More and more people around the world are getting to know the outstanding qualities of this fine breed.

HISTORY OF THE
FINNISH LAPPHUND

The Finnish Lapphund is both a new and old breed: new, in that it has only been formally recognised as a breed since 1945, when the first breed standard was produced; and old, because dogs of this type are synonymous with reindeer farmers. Cave paintings and early writings show that there have been Arctic spitz breeds in Lapland since 7000 BC. Originally, the dogs would have been a guarding/hunting breed, able to protect the reindeer herds and at the same time hunt for food, no doubt for their own survival and perhaps as an added bonus to their reindeer-farming families. The hunting instinct is still very evident in many of today's Finnish Lapphunds.

As the relationship between man and dog developed, the dog's herding instincts became greatly valued and dogs with strong herding skills proved of added value to the farmers, who would breed his best working dogs instead of other dogs. The early reindeer-herding dogs were very important to the reindeer farmers, the dogs being elevated to family-member status. Likewise, a good

Puuranvaara Cerniila, a true working dog from the Finnish Lapphund-Paimensukuinen line.

herding dog was considered a measure of wealth.

For the early dogs, there was no uniformity in terms of their outward appearance and breed type; instead, they were grouped by their ability to work with the reindeer farmers and their ability to survive. With the reindeer farmers and their dogs covering a large geographical area (Lapland, covering northern Sweden, Norway and Finland), the dogs' type would vary, just as opinions on what made a good dog would vary. Thus, the general appearance and colour could be quite diverse, though the nature of the work and terrain would have ensured that a number of similarities existed across all of the dogs being used for reindeer herding.

In the old Saame writings, there was only one general type of reindeer dog—long in body, somewhat rectangular in shape, with long hair and a straight tail except on the move, when the tail curled up. The colour was very varied, with black with 'four eyes' being the most common (reference to the tricolour markings seen today). Other colours like red and brown were considered beautiful. The mottled white did exist, but pure white was not popular as it made it difficult to distinguish the dogs in the snow. Grey was not favoured either, as it was the colour of wolves.

In the 1700s, Carl von Linné and Georges Louis de Buffon categorised the native dogs of Scandinavia into two main

History

groups: the *Pystykorva* (spitz), which were erect-eared dogs like the Finnish Spitz; and the *Paimenkoira*, which were the herding dogs. In later years (1868 and 1871), during treks to Lapland, Professor Gustaf von Duben noted that the Lap reindeer farmers used herding dogs, which could be either long- or short-coated. In 1895, the Russian Olenov compared these dogs to the Eskimo dogs, but the herding dogs were much smaller in size and shorter legged.

The war years and the following distemper epidemic had a very devastating effect on these native dogs, and their numbers diminished drastically. After the war, the Finnish Kennel Club created a breed called the Lappish Herder. The size was defined as 52–56 cms (20–22 ins) for dogs and 49–53 cms (19.25–21 ins) for bitches. These Lappish dogs were named *Kukonharjulainen*, the cockhill type after the main breeder of the time, the kennel Kukonharjun. It is believed that these dogs were produced by crossing the herding dogs with the black and white Karelian Bear Dogs. The resultant dogs were usually black, big and long, with a slim skull similar to that of the black Belgian Shepherd (Groenendael). They also lacked the coat of an Arctic dog. This type of dog was a man-made creation, not truly descended from the original Lapland dogs. Today it would be extremely rare to see any of these Kukonharjulainen dogs in the pedigrees of our modern Lapphunds, as they were largely ignored when the ancestors of today's dogs were brought down from Lapland.

In the 1950s, the Finnish Kennel Association (Finland's second major kennel organisation) started to create a breed that was called the Lapponian Herder, which was based on the indigenous reindeer-herding-dog population. The standard of the time quotes the height to be 52–56

REINDEER HERDERS

The Finnish Lapphund was originally bred to herd reindeer in northern Finland. The advance of the use of the motor sled/snowmobile in the wintertime has meant that the dogs are more commonly seen now as family pets than as working dogs. Nevertheless, many breeders continue to promote the working aspects of the breed.

12 FINNISH LAPPHUND

Top: Peera, working reindeer.
Bottom: Peera, at ten years of age, a true working dog from the Finnish Lapphund-Paimensukuinen line.

History

The Karelian Bear Dog is believed to have been crossed with reindeer-herding dogs to create the Lappish Herder in Finland.

cms (20.5–22 ins) for dogs and 49–53 cms (19.25–21 ins) for bitches, and the acceptable colours were defined as black, bear-brown and white. White markings on the feet, chest, throat and tip of tail, plus the familiar brown spots above the eyes, on the legs and under the tail were also accepted. However, grey or red colours were considered to be faults.

During the years 1959–1961, dogs in the northern reindeer-farming area were scrutinised by official inspectors of the Lappish Kennel District, the Finnish Spitz Organisation and the Finnish Kennel Association, so that the dogs could be categorised under the aforementioned types.

FINNISH LAPPHUND

Notice the differences between the Lapponian Herder, shown here, and the Finnish Lapphund in shape and angulation. The coat is not the only difference that separates the two breeds.

Head study of a Lapponian Herder (Lapinporokoira).

The Finnish kennel organisations became unified in the early 1960s to form the Finnish Kennel Club, and all of the different Lapphund dogs from all over Finland that were registered with different organisations were accepted into the same breed register (the Y-register). Problems resulted as breeders came to realise that some lines had become shorter coated, while others were definitely long-coated.

The future of the Lappish breeds was reassessed in 1967, and the dogs were separated at shows solely on the basis of their coat lengths. However, this did

> **LAPPONIAN COUSINS**
> The Finnish Lapphund and Lapponian Herder were originally considered to be the same breed. The two breeds were separated in the 1960s, and separate standards defined for each.

not fully resolve the issues of type within the breed, so the Finnish Kennel Club decided to transfer the Finnish Lapphunds to the X-register. It was still possible that dogs brought to the south from Lapland could be accepted into this X-register.

The breed register in Finland is still open, allowing 'natural' unregistered dogs to be admitted to the breed if they meet the standard. This enables breeders to add new bloodlines from the Saame farmers. The dogs must be of true Lapland breed descent and of proven working origins, evaluated by a panel of experts to be 'natural' dogs and certified as true Finnish Lapphunds. One such dog turned out to be a sire of tremendous impact on the breed's gene pool in the UK: Runne (20099/93), a sire introduced to the Lecibsin kennel (from the Norway region of Lapland) in the mid-1990s, became the sire of the UK import Lec. Hankka at Leemax.

Once the breed had been differentiated by coat length, the breeds were actually split in the 1960s, with the short-coated Lapponian Herder (Lapin-porokoira) receiving its first official pedigree in 1966, and the Finnish Lapphund being distinguished as a separate breed in 1967. It is interesting to note that the way the reindeer farmers worked began to change at this time. Skidoos began to replace dogs in reindeer herding and the longhaired dogs were no longer considered ideal by the farmer. More often the dogs selected to work alongside the skidoos were of the short-coated variety.

Although the reindeer farmers no longer favoured the longhaired Lapphund, there were others who sought to preserve the breed for families to enjoy in the south. In the 1970s, a new era in breeding started with relatively strong, short and wide-headed dogs with rough, standing coats, which were found in Lapland. Marri Vainio of the Peski kennel is credited with identifying many of these animals from Lapland, as is the Poromiehen kennel.

Herding dogs were no longer used in eastern Lapland, and it was only in the far northwest of Finnish Lapland where dogs were still used in the traditional way. Marri had a good knowledge of the dogs and the dog families of Lapland, and selected individuals with as pure a background as was still possible, demonstrating the breed type of the traditional

16 FINNISH LAPPHUND

An example of old Peski lines: the bitch Kuuki (Peski Naappu x Peski Naattu).

Finnish Ch Peski Tsahpi (Peski Muste x Peski Muotka).

Lapland herding dog. The pedigrees of two Peski-bred dogs, Peski Muste and Peski Koira, show the key dogs of the time, Runne, Ceepu and Velho Huli. The registration numbers were prefixed by 'X-' to show the time when the dogs were taken to the central breed register.

The breed standard was approved in 1975. The ideal size range was defined as 49–55 cms (19.25–21.5 ins) for dogs and 43–49 cms (17–19.25 ins) for bitches. It should be noted that size has continued to be reduced, as further revisions of the standard have been made, with the latest standard quoting 46–52 cms (18–20.5 ins) for dogs and 41–47 cms (16–18.5 ins) for bitches. When the standard was revised in 1993, the name was changed from Lapinkoira to Suomenlapinkoira.

During the 1970s, a number of key sires were introduced to the breeding programmes: Kalikkakaula (X-11/78) was registered in 1978, SF MVA Fredi (SF-27143T/76) in 1976 and Multi Ch Lecibsin Torsti (22374S/77) in 1977. Kalikkakaula is noted as being of unknown parentage on the Finnish Breed Register, but it is known that he was the son of a registered Swedish Lapphund, Tsorni, bred by Juhls and Broome in Kautokeino, Norway.

Breeders soon noticed that the length of the coat was not the only difference between the two breeds known as the Finnish Lapphund and the Lapponian Herder. Other differences included the length-to-height ratio, angulation and tail set. Through the 1980s, the breeds began to differ more in these areas, and the breed we recognise as today's Finnish Lapphund emerged. Today there is no question that the Finnish Lapphund and Lapponian Herder are two different breeds. Having said that, one must acknowledge that there have been and will be dogs in both breeds that are longer or shorter in body and/or coat than their standards allow, which

Sarumen, Peera, Cerniila and Narya, from the Pukranveera kennel, pulling the *pulka* (sleigh).

Swedish Lapphund.

FINNISH CLUBS
There are two clubs in Finland that have responsibility for the breed, the *Lappalaiskoirat ry*, which also includes the Lapponian Herder (Lapinporokoira) and the Swedish Lapphund (Ruotsinlapinkoira), and the *Paimensukuisen Lapinkoiran Seura*.

only proves that the breeds share a common origin. The *Lappalaiskoirat ry* (Lapphund Club of Finland) was established in 1970 and registered in 1971, and covers the interests of Lapponian Herders, Swedish Lapphunds and Finnish Lapphunds.

The story does not end there, as there were many people who believed that these 'new' Lapphunds were too short and too heavily coated. They wanted to have a type of Finnish Lapphund that was more akin in type to its short-coated relative, the Lapponian Herder. Within this group of breeders, there are those who believe that only these lines are from proven herding stock, and that the modern Finnish Lapphund is not. The author disputes this, since we know that both are derived from actual working dogs brought down from Lapland, and the Peski dogs are seen throughout many Lapphund pedigrees, be they 'working' or 'show' type. However, by selective breeding from a restricted pool of some 29-stem dogs, this group of people developed a breed within the Finnish Lapphund breed called *Paimensukuinen Lapinkoira*, which simply translates as 'working Finnish Lapphunds.' The dogs of the 'working lines' are perhaps less uniform in type, and within the group no single colour is favoured; practically no colour is deemed to be a fault. There have been a number of attempts to separate the types as different breeds without success.

Of course, when you look back through the generations of pedigrees of all of the Lapphunds, you will see that both Finnish Lapphunds and Paimensukuinen Lapinkoira share the same ancestry (along with the Lapponian Herder), and that type and working ability vary through both factions of the breed. The simple fact that the current-day show dogs were also developed from dogs brought down from Lapland, of which many were reindeer herders, shows that their working ability also must be present. The Aarnipuro line of Jakke Aarnipuro included the black male Musti (79304/81) who was working as a reindeer herder but also went on to become a show champion. Many of today's show dogs resemble him in type.

The *Paimensukuinen Lapinkoiran Seura* (Society for the Original Reindeer Herder) was founded in 1981 and seeks to preserve these Paimensukuinen lines, independent of the other Finnish Lapphunds. In 2000, approximately 120 Paimensukuinen puppies were born in Finland out of the total 700-plus Finnish Lapphunds registered with the Finnish Kennel Club.

Under the PEVISA system in Finland, all breeding stock must be health-screened before being used in breeding programmes. The hips are x-rayed and scored on a range of A to E (A being good, E being poor), and the eyes are tested for signs of progressive retinal atrophy (PRA) and hereditary cataracts (HC). This routine testing of eyes did not really start until many of the key dogs had been heavily used at stud, and the subsequent identification of a number of PRA-affected animals then had a large impact on the breeding programmes of many kennels both at in Finland and abroad. In 2001, from approximately 2402 Finnish Lapphunds tested in Finland, 2.25% were identified with PRA and 3.41% with HC.

The Finnish Lapphund Club of Finland (*Lappalaiskoirat ry*) maintains a list of all health test results. Pedigrees of all PRA- and HC-affected animals are routinely reported in the club's yearbooks. Affected animals are noted by adding the abbreviation PRA or HC after the name, e.g. Lecibsin Torsti PRA. In the case of PRA, as

The Swedish Lapphund is also a spitz-type herding breed, developed in the Swedish region of Lapland.

Multi Ch Lecibsin Torsti.

FINNISH LAPPHUND

The UK's first import, the bitch Lecibsin Loru at Sulyka.

Multi Ch Lecibsin Hissukka was imported in whelp to the UK, where she produced an important litter before returning home to Finland. She is shown here as a veteran in Finland.

the method of inheritance is believed to be through a simple recessive gene, both parents of an affected animal and any offspring are known to be carriers. These are similarly noted by an asterisk after their name, e.g. Kalikkakaula*.

THE FINNISH LAPPHUND IN THE UK

The story started in 1989, when Roger and Sue Dunger (Sulyka kennel) fell in love with the breed while on a trip to Finland. They imported the first Lapphund from the successful Lecibsin kennels, this being the bitch Lecibsin Loru. Loru was to become the UK's foundation bitch. At this time, the UK was subject to strict quarantine regulations for dogs imported, and it was decided that a sensible way to increase numbers and bloodlines was to import a bitch in whelp through quarantine. The Dungers took the advice of Jukka Kuusisto of the Lecibsin kennels and were very fortunate to be able to 'borrow' the top-winning bitch of the time, Multi Ch Lecibsin Hissukka, who was mated to Finnish Ch Fohrmans Hermanni. Hissukka only stayed briefly in quarantine, to whelp and wean her litter of five pups, before returning to Finland to continue her winning show career. From this litter came the tricoloured male Sulyka Lecibsin Nilla, who was mated to Loru, to produce a number of key Lapphunds in the UK.

Their first litter in November 1992 produced the striking tricoloured bitch Sulyka Mischa at Elbereth (owned by author Toni Jackson of the Elbereth kennels); Mischa became the top-winning Lapphund in the UK. Mischa has also been shown in Finland and was graded excellent and awarded a Certificate quality ribbon. At the Belgium International show in

2001, Mischa was awarded the CAC/CACIB at nine years of age.

From a subsequent repeat mating of Nilla to Loru, the tricoloured male Sulyka Valio is Curdeleon (owned by J and P Chetwynd of the Curdeleon kennel) was born. Along with the author's Mischa, he dominated the show ring in the 1990s and became the breed's top-winning male. From these two matings, no less than seven dogs/bitches were awarded Best of Sex or Best of Breed awards at major UK shows, to ensure Loru and Nilla were the UK's Top Rare Breed Brood Bitch and Stud Dog throughout the mid- to late 1990s.

Further importations in the mid-1990s included the brown and tan dog Staalon Runne of Sulyka and the black and tan dog Tsinghuan Poarka at Chelville, plus three bitches—the cream Shezadun Abjatar at Chelville, the red sable Kutrin Lumo at Chelville and the wolf sable Lecibsin Hanka at Leemax. Runne was to become the breed's most popular sire of the 1990s, siring nine different litters, but sadly one of the resultant pups was diagnosed with suspected PRA. With a similar suspected case found in a bitch produced by the first Loru x Nilla mating, this diagnosis meant that UK breeders had to think carefully about future breeding programmes.

The new imports brought additional colours to the gene pool, which meant that breeders were now able to produce a wide variety of the colours seen in the breed. Shezadun Abjatar at Chelville (imported by Mr and Mrs C Muzzelle of the Chelville kennels) produced the successful cream male, Chelville Saame, who was the breed's first cream to be awarded a Best of Sex award at a major UK show. In 1999, the Muzzelles imported two further bitches, the Finnish Ch Eetla and

A well-known and influential sire in the UK, Sulyka Lecibsin Nilla.

Staalon Runne of Sulyka, photographed in quarantine, was imported into the UK.

Staalon Kidda. Eetla came into quarantine, having been mated in Finland to Orso Farm Maahinen and whelped a litter of four.

Happily arriving later, Staalon Kidda came under the Balai directive. Eetla was a different colour again to that already seen in the UK, being more black/bear brown with the eye rim spectacles often seen in the breed. Two of her progeny from this litter, Chelville Tapio and Chelville Eija, were later to return to Finland for a short time, where they earned their Finnish championship titles. By the end of the 1990s, the breed numbers in the UK were just over 150.

In February 2000, the UK's quarantine regulations were re-examined and the government introduced an alternative method for importing rabies-free stock to the UK, a scheme named the Pet Passport Scheme. This scheme enabled dogs that had been microchipped, rabies-vaccinated and blood-tested to be imported to the UK without the need for a six-month quarantine, provided that six months had passed since the relevant blood test. This scheme was a more attractive way of introducing dogs to the UK.

The first pioneer of this scheme for the breed was the bitch Sulyka Mischa at Elbereth, who flew to Finland in February 2000 to be mated to Finnish Ch Lumiturpa Nörri (owned by Matti Takanen). Mischa returned home after the mating and duly produced a litter of eight puppies in the UK.

The wolf sable bitch, Lumiturpa Seita (Glenchess kennels); the wolf sable dog, Shacal Kehu (Pennardane kennels); the red sable dog, Lapinlumon Esikuva (Carlacot kennels) and the tricoloured dog, Finnish Ch Heldalan Fidel (Hildrek kennels) were imported under the Pet Passport Scheme in 2001, further increasing the bloodlines available in the UK. Fidel was later identified with PRA, so he will not be used at stud in the UK, but the two young males have already started to be used as sires. By 2001, the UK's population of Finnish Lapphunds had passed 180. Two dogs bred in the UK have been exported, one to Australia and one to Holland, and there are also a number of Lapphunds living in Ireland.

In May 1994, a small band of enthusiasts founded The Finnish Lapphund Club of Great Britain, and in November 1995 the club was provisionally recognised by The Kennel Club. The club's aim is to protect and further the interests of the breed in the UK.

THE FINNISH LAPPHUND IN DENMARK
The first Finnish Lapphund arrived in Denmark in 1982. Turid Uthaug, who had been involved

The author, Toni Jackson of Elbereth Kennels, with one of her winning Finnish Lapphunds.

in breeding Lapphunds in Lapland, had lived there for many years and helped Marri Vainio collect dogs for the famous Peski kennel breeding programme. Indeed, Turid was in Finland when it all began with this breed, so, when she moved to Denmark, she imported about 15 dogs from the Peski kennels. Her kennel name, Koira, means 'dog' in Finnish, and under this name about 100 Finnish Lapphunds were bred until she stopped in the late 1980s. Thanks to her efforts, breeders in Denmark had a very good foundation for the breed from one of the oldest kennels in Finland.

Two other kennels started at nearly the same time, also with imports from the Peski kennels. Of course, other breeders based their foundation stock on dogs from the kennel Koira, but it was not until the early 1990s that the breed became more well known and several new breeders came along, and more dogs started to attend the shows and get noticed.

This meant that obviously all of the foundation dogs in the breed were of the old Peski line. Although more recent imports from Finland cannot be traced back to this line, it is fair to say that nearly all Danish dogs have a lot of Peski blood in them, and many are pure Peski. It is interesting to note that, unlike in Finland, where some of the kennels with the Peski line founded their own club and split away from other lines (resulting in *Paimensukuisen linja* /working lines), the breeders in Denmark chose to work with all of the dogs available to reach their goal of breeding correct Lapphunds.

This means that Denmark has many dogs that represent valuable bloodlines for the breed, even in Finland where many of these lines do not exist any longer or are six or more generations back. For this reason, there has been interest in Danish dogs in Finland and no fewer than eight dogs have been exported back to the country of origin. This indeed is a high compliment to the Danish breeders when you consider that there are far fewer Lapphunds in Denmark as compared to Finland.

The first eight dogs imported were Lapinlumon Aslan, Lapinlumon Darius, Lapinlumon Festivitas, Lapinlumon Gievra, Lapinlumon Gaisa, Finda Fabian, Kello Reijo and Kello Riina. The most important of these so far have been Lapinlumon Aslan and Kello Reijo, both of whom have sired many litters and have puppies all over the world. Aslan's pups can be found in Norway, Sweden, Holland, Switzerland and other countries, and Reijo has several puppies in Sweden, one which is building the foundation for the breed in Australia and beyond.

During the early years in Denmark, the breed was not exhibited much at dog shows, as Turid Uthaug was not a great believer in shows. She felt that these dogs were intended for working and, since that was how she had gotten to know them in Lapland, that was how she wanted them to remain. Nevertheless, her daughter did show one of their males, Ch Peski Nolla, to his title through outings at very few shows. Besides Nolla, her dogs really have not been shown.

The breed's top winner in those years was Ch Salto Tundra (owned by Mrs Kirsten Graungaard of the kennel Tranemosen), who is also the father of Aslan. Tundra also went on to claim the World Winner title in 1989. In 1991, a new import arrived from Finland, Ch Matsi (owned by Mr Georg Carlsen of the kennel Inari). This was the beginning of a new time for the breed in Denmark because, until then, the majority of the dogs in the country were of the Peski line. Matsi was not from a show line, though, after him, several others arrived. Matsi was the breed's top winner for some years in the early 1990s and he sired many puppies.

In 1994, a new import arrived from Finland who became the breed's all-time top winner in Denmark, Ch Fidelis Uuriel (owned by Miss Sarah Brandes of the kennel Lapinlumon). In 1997, he became the first Danish-owned Lapphund to achieve the International Championship title. Later, the first Danish-owned bitch was awarded her International Championship title, the bitch being Inari Rinku, a puppy from Matsi. Fidelis Uuriel was also the first Finnish Lapphund to be awarded a Best in Show (BIS) award at an all-breed show in Denmark, this historic event occurring in November 2001 at Herning International with about 3000 dogs entered under Finnish judge Hans Lehtinen. This was a great achievement for the Finnish Lapphund. At the International show in 2002, he won top honours again, from more than 50 veterans of all breeds, with the

Danish Ch Salto Tundra is an example of Peski dogs: Peski Seppo x Peski Nätti.

FINNISH LAPPHUND

English judge Zena Thorn Andrews picking him as BIS3. Hopefully this is a sign that the Finnish Lapphund will slowly get more attention from the judges all over the world.

In the new century, a new winning dog has come to the fore, a beautiful imported bitch from Finland named Lumiturpa Saana (owned by Mrs Margit Gottorp of the kennel Gottorp and bred by Matti Takanen). She has done very well thus far in the show ring.

Denmark has been lucky to have very healthy breeding stock. There have been some cases of hereditary cataracts and only one incidence of PRA, this recorded in a bitch imported from the Lecibsin kennels, but fortunately both she and her puppies were removed from the breeding programme and no further cases have been recorded since.

The majority of dogs x-rayed have good hips. Denmark has the same scoring system as Finland and most dogs tested have A or B scores. Some poorer scores have been seen, but there does not appear to be a problem with hips in the breed.

All breed colours are seen in Denmark, and many of the first dogs imported by the kennel Koira were brown or wolf-grey. Yet, since then, all colours have been seen in the breeding stock, even blue! The breed's top winner, Fidelis Uuriel, is black and white, and a successful bitch,

Danish dog Koira Lempi at 10 years of age. He is the offspring of Peski Koira DK (of Denmark, not the same dog as Finnish Ch Peski Koira) and Peski Kulta.

the import Ch Fidelis Dana (top-winning bitch for one year), is red.

Fortunately, no judges have ever criticised the colours of these successful dogs. In more recent years, many wolf-grey puppies have been born and it seems that people in Denmark generally appreciate the great variety of colours in this breed. About 50 puppies are registered each year, so it is still not a popular breed in Denmark, but the breed is getting more popular and numbers are increasing steadily. So, after 20 years in Denmark, this breed is definitely there to stay.

THE FINNISH LAPPHUND IN THE UNITED STATES

Like the UK, the US has its own kennel club and does not automatically recognise breeds accepted by the Fédération Cynologique Internationale (FCI). Currently, the Finnish Lapphund is not recognised by the American Kennel Club (AKC), and Linda Marden (Sugarok kennels) has maintained the breed registry. The breed is now on the AKC Foundation Stock Service (FSS) but unfortunately cannot compete at AKC shows. Other societies, however, such as the American Rare Breed Association (ARBA), do accept the breed.

While it is understood that a few Lapphunds went to the US when their owners migrated there, these dogs were not registered in the US and no organised attempt was made until 1987, when Linda Marden started to import. Linda first learned about the breed in 1977 while reading an article in a Samoyed magazine, the breed with which she was then involved. Following considerable research into both the Swedish and Finnish Lapphund, Linda, along with Madelin Druse, decided to import the Finnish Lapphund. The first two dogs imported, in early 1987, were Fohrman's Kukka and Fohrman's Kimmo, littermates (female and male) sired by Fin Ch Lecibsin Hurra out of Likka. Kukka was owned by Madelin and Kimmo was owned by Gae Crose. Kimmo was originally destined for Linda, but circumstances prohibited her from accepting him at the time.

In the fall of 1987, Sugarok received their first Lapphunds, Jesse (a dog by Fin Ch Naavapirtin

Another of Peski Koira DK's offspring is Koira Nasti, pictured at 13 years of age.

Mitali x Seita, bred by Marie Kallio) and Mocha (a bitch named Fohrman's Ninni, by Fin Ch. Lecibsin Hurraa x Tytto). Mocha was owned by Karen McFarlane.

Shortly after importing these dogs, it was learned that Lecibsin Hurraa was a carrier of PRA. All of the Lapphunds in the US were examined as they aged, and none was found to have PRA. This was a fortunate situation, and care was taken never to double on Hurraa in the Sugarok breeding programme. So far, no Finnish Lapphund in America has been diagnosed with PRA, but the condition is no doubt inevitable.

Two littersisters, Salto Panda and Salto Prosa (by Seppo x Peski Naetti, bred by Helga Haarbo and all Peski background), were also imported in 1987. Panda went to Madelin and Prosa went to Gae Crose. Sadly, Prosa was diagnosed with retinal folds and by then Kimmo had developed cataracts, so they were never bred from. However, Kimmo was shown extensively to help promote the breed.

Additionally in 1987, Madelin imported the female Fohrman's Outi (by Ch Lecibsin Hurraa x Fohrman's Arla, bred by Valfrid Kling) and the male Orso-Farm Jeti (by Ch Mettanpeikon Hoppu x Orso-Farm Calicca, bred by Eija Lehtimaki).

The first American-bred puppy was born on 16 October 1988 from Fohrman's Kukka and Orso-Farm Jeti. The second litter was at Sugarok, from Mocha mated to Jesse.

The next importations were Kutrin Elli-Noora (a bitch bred by Suzanna and Sauli Savela), Omani Otsu-Pieti (a dog bred by Sakari Viinamaki) and Pasifixin Vayry (a dog bred by Kari Schonroos). Pieti went to live with Sharon Kremsreiter, though he unfortunately turned out to be sterile, which was especially disappointing as he is a rich brown colour. Vayry turned out to be a very special dog at Sugarok; he was shown extensively in the newly organised ARBA dog shows and garnered many outstanding wins. Sadly, Vayry died in 1997, still in the prime of his life, after drinking some antifreeze. His death had a great impact on Linda, and she nearly decided to give up the breed.

Luckily for the Finnish Lapphund in the US, the Sugarok kennels decided to carry on and have been promoting the breed successfully. Further influential imports to the Sugarok kennels during 1999 and 2000 have included the Finnish Ch males Fidelis Roastil and Staalon Halitulijalla, and the bitches Fidelis Naruska and Orso Farm Loddi. Other breeders active in the US include the Burkwalls, who bred a litter in November 1999 from their Sugarok Lappland

Mr R Vuorinen judging Ch Sarki Fény Uimakoulun Kuhomo at the World Dog Show in Amsterdam.

with Love mated with fresh semen imported from Finland from the Fin Ch Kotikulman Onnenoikku.

Now that the breed has been accepted to the FSS, it is hoped that more litters will be produced to establish the breed in the US and to enable progression to full AKC recognition within the coming years. There were 160 Finnish Lapphunds on the registry handed over to the AKC.

THE FINNISH LAPPHUND IN HOLLAND
The first Finnish Lapphund arrived in Holland in 1985, the male Lecibsin Cesky. He was followed in 1987 by the first bitch, Lecibsin Leija. These dogs were never used for breeding due to the

risks PRA associated with the dogs Lecibsin Torsti and Lecibsin Kosma, both of whom were in the pedigrees of these early imports. The year 1992 saw the arrival of Fidelis Larissa and Lecibsin Aapeli, with the bitch Fidelis Quirina Vartija being imported in 1993. Fidelis Quirina Vartija became the first Dutch champion for the breed.

There were originally three breeders in Holland: kennel Lumipyri, kennel v.d. Nieuwenkamp and kennel Sarky Feny. The first litter was born to Lecibsin Larissa x Lecibsin Aapeli, and in 1995 the Sarky Feny kennel, bred from Fidelis Quirina Vartija x Lecibsin Reinikainen. Further importations at the time included the bitches Terhakan Juotiki and Fidelis Xanthia Pulkka. In 1996, the male Leemax Hollantielle was imported from England and the bitch Nutukas Unikukka was imported from Finland. In 1998, Lecibsin Aapeli was again eye-tested and was found to be affected with PRA, meaning that the first litter would all be carriers of the condition.

There have been many imports to Holland in recent years, including some 19 dogs in 1999 and a further 18 in 2000. These Lapphunds were imported from Finland, Sweden, Denmark and France, with much care taken to ensure that the imported dogs came from a wide range of bloodlines to give future breeders more possibilities when looking for suitable combinations. Before breeding, the parents are scored for hip dysplasia and are eye-tested. Thus far, in addition to the one case of PRA, a number of cataracts have been identified.

In the first 16 years of the breed in Holland, only 10 litters have been produced. These litters, combined with the imports, have produced over 100 Finnish Lapphunds in Holland. The Finnish Lapphund belongs to SCANDIA, the Dutch club for breeders and fanciers of the Scandinavian dog breeds, but it is hoped that the Dutch Finnish Lapphund enthusiasts will soon have their own breed club, which could gain official status.

THE FINNISH LAPPHUND IN THE REST OF EUROPE

The Finnish Lapphund is seen throughout Europe with many successful kennels existing in Sweden, Norway, Switzerland and France. Dogs from these countries move reasonably freely to enable matings, importations, loans and showing to take place, allowing the breed to develop successfully, as has been the case in Denmark and Holland.

THE FINNISH LAPPHUND IN AUSTRALIA

Kylikki Eronen (of Brambleway Kennels in Canberra) was the

History

first person to introduce the Finnish Lapphund to Australia. In 1995, she imported a solid black bitch from the Sulyka kennels in England and, in 1997, she imported a brown male from Staalon kennels in Finland, Staalon Kolumbus (by Multi Ch Hiekkaniemen Livari x Staalon Tinttarella). Unfortunately, attempts to breed from this pair were unsuccessful. A subsequent attempt to mate the Sulyka bitch by using semen imported from Finland was also thwarted when the semen was lost in transit.

In 2000, Kylikki imported a black and tan bitch from Finland, Lecibsin Heissulivei (Lecibsin Tino x Lecibsin Hurja Hilta) and in April 2001 the first litter of three puppies was successfully born in Australia, from Lecibsin Heissulivei to Staalon Kolumbus.

In August 2001, the Theldaroy kennels of Ros and Col Seare (Queensland) imported another breeding pair from Finland—a black and tan male from Staalon kennels, Staalon Bestseller (Fin Ch Kello Reijo x Fin Ch Staalon Silba), and a black and tan bitch from Tositouhun kennels, Tositouhun Eve Example (Fin Ch Suursaaren Huura x Tositouhun Arlene). These two were mated and in December 2001 the breed numbers were increased by a further seven. The breed has been well accepted into the Australian show ring, with many notable successes.

Winners at the World Show in Helsinki. Left: Best of Opposite Sex Multi Ch Menninkäisen Aikaovela (male) and right: Best of Breed Fin Est Ch Lumiturpa Juulia (female).

CHARACTERISTICS OF THE
FINNISH LAPPHUND

One of the National Dogs of Finland, the Finnish Lapphund is a medium-sized spitz of a very friendly nature, with a keenness for learning. The Lapphund is strongly built and capable of a day's work herding reindeer. Characteristics and temperament are accurately summarised in the English breed standard: 'Tendency to herd, intelligent, brave, calm, faithful, suitable as companion and watchdog.' Only those fortunate enough to be Finnish Lapphund owners will know just how typical that description is of the breed. The breed works in Lapland to this day as a herder of reindeer. It is described by the Lapps as a galloping dog and it works alongside the Lapponian Herder, a trotting dog. Between them, the two breeds are said to work the herds ideally, their styles perfectly complementing each other.

The breed's origins with the nomadic people of northern Finland meant that dogs were valued according to their ability and willingness to work with the reindeer. The more able dogs were obviously highly prized and bred from, creating a sensible and intelligent breed with a fondness for people and a willingness to work. The old writings show that the Lapp people thought highly of their dogs, letting them sleep with them and often feeding the dogs before they fed themselves. This has resulted in a breed that is very people-oriented; this characteristic is easily seen in its very genuine temperament. Unlike the more

A REAL OUTDOOR DOG
The Finnish Lapphund is one of only two breeds permitted to be kennelled outside during the winter months in Finland (the Lapponian Herder being the other breed). The breed is capable of surviving the extreme cold of a harsh Finnish winter.

familiar herding breed, the Border Collie, the Lapphund does not see a need to be owned by one master; instead, it chooses to be owned by a whole family and is willing to share its affections with all members of the family.

Being fairly wild in its origins, the breed still retains a robust health and is fairly long-lived. Some hereditary conditions have been seen, but the breed in general is very healthy and can be considered 'low-maintenance.'

HEALTH CONCERNS IN LAPPHUNDS

The breed is a naturally healthy breed, not suffering from any documented major health problems. This vigour is probably related to its fairly wild background, being descended no doubt on a 'survival of the fittest' principle through many generations of working dogs. The Saame reindeer farmers would not have retained unhealthy strains of dogs. Life expectancy is around 12 to 14 years, but dogs of 16 to 17 years of age are not uncommon in Finland. The author has seen many 15-year-old-plus dogs still enjoying their lives and living outside in the snow.

There are two conditions that are seen in the breed and should be highlighted. Both conditions are hereditary eye defects that have been recorded in the breed in its home country of Finland and in other countries as well.

GENERALISED PROGRESSIVE RETINAL ATROPHY (GPRA)

This is an hereditary eye disease that affects many breeds. As the name suggests, it is a progressive disease in which affected dogs can become totally blind. The condition is usually noticed when owners first become aware of a loss of night vision in their dogs. The condition then progresses over time to a loss of vision in all types of lighting. It is believed that the condition is inherited via a simple autosomal recessive gene; therefore, where the condition is noted, the parents and offspring of any affected animal must themselves be carriers of the condition, even if not affected themselves.

The biggest problem relating to this condition in our breed is the age of onset. There has been a wide range of ages when the condition has been first noticed, anywhere from one to eight years of age (even in dogs that have received regular annual eye tests). In a situation where a dog has tested as free of the condition until about five years of age, followed by a positive failure, there is a reasonable chance that by that time the now-proven affected animal has produced offspring that themselves will be carriers and may in many cases have gone onto produce further litters.

In Finland, under the PEVISA health schemes, breeding stock must have a valid eye certificate that is no more than two years old.

This ruling by the Finnish Kennel Club helps to identify affected dogs and enable breeders to remove them from their breeding programmes. The Kennel Club does not operate such a scheme in the UK, but breeders who are members of the Finnish Lapphund Club of Great Britain operate under a Code of Ethics whereby they ensure that the eye test certificates on their breeding stock are no more than one year old.

Eradication by breeding alone is difficult in a condition that cannot be detected before breeding age is reached. Of course, affected animals and known carriers must be removed from future breeding programmes, thus helping to reduce the incidence of the condition. However, until such a time when we have identified the DNA markers for this condition and a blood test for screening pups is available, it will not be possible to prevent hidden carriers from being used in breeding.

It is important to note that in most cases the progression to total blindness is slow and the effect on the dog's daily life can be only minimal. The dog's other key senses are able to compensate such that the blind dog may not appear to be handicapped when in his familiar surroundings.

Hereditary Cataracts

There are many types of cataracts, the condition being defined as any opacity of the lens or the lens capsule. Since cataracts can be caused by a number of factors, identifying the actual cause of a cataract is very difficult. Causes of cataracts may be due to congenital abnormality, *in utero* infection, trauma or injury to the eye or metabolic disorders, or produced as a result of nutritional disorders or by the influence of certain drugs. Yet cataracts seen in many breeds have proven to be hereditary, and since the incidence in Finnish Lapphunds in their homeland has been significant, Finnish vets and breeders have elected to regard some cataracts as hereditary. At present, this is not the case in the US or UK, where the number of cases is small.

The Finns have yet to identify the mode of inheritance of these cataracts and believe it to be far more complex than the simple autosomal recessive gene of PRA. Therefore, parents and offspring are not deemed to be carriers unless a parent produces more than one cataract-affected offspring in different litters.

GENERAL BREED DESCRIPTION

Undoubtedly the Finnish Lapphund has many spitz features, complimented by its attractive heavy coat and its intelligence. It is a well-balanced dog of athletic build, medium size and excellent temperament. These features have led to the breed's becoming a very popular pet in its native Finland, with growing popularity in many other countries. Its athleticism and keenness to learn means it is good for the lively family but perhaps not so well-suited to a sedentary way of life. However, while the breed does demonstrate some spitz characteristics, it should be stressed that the breed should not develop into a showy heavy-coated spitz, standing with its tail up all the time, but should be a more primitive animal that should bear some similarities to the rough and tough wolverine.

TEMPERAMENT AND ABILITIES

As a breed that has evolved with close ties to people, working with and for people, its keenness to live with and please its owners is not surprising. The Finnish Lapphund is a very intelligent breed, and this factor must not be overlooked when deciding if the breed is suitable for you. The breed is well respected as a family pet in Finland and its popularity rose throughout the 1990s, where it was among the 15 most popular breeds in Finland. In the new century, the breed reached the number 8 position in registration popularity with 704 dogs registered.

The breed makes a good watchdog, but not necessarily a good guard dog. Its keen hearing and alert nature ensure that it will never miss anything, but the breed's friendly nature means that it

Wolverine of the species *Gulo luscus*. The Finnish Lapphund has some primitive traits that can be compared to those of the wolverine.

cannot necessarily be relied upon to protect your property.

The trainability of the breed can be demonstrated in the versatility of the jobs and hobbies that it enjoys. Perhaps one of the greatest ambassadors for the breed is "Tara," the first fully trained support dog working for Dogs for the Disabled. Tara is an invaluable friend and helper to her disabled companion, Norma Cail. Her talents include loading the washing machine, tidying up, helping undress Norma and putting her to bed. As well as the trained tasks that Tara can do, she is also an important friend and social aid to Norma—wheelchair users are often ignored, but once people see Tara, these barriers are broken. In a similar vein, a young Lapphund is currently in training as a demonstration dog for Hearing Dogs for the Deaf—he will be taught to alert his handler to any household noises, such as alarms, crying babies and the telephone ringing.

These two specific examples demonstrate the sheer trainability of the breed, and so it will be no surprise to hear that the Finnish Lapphund can be trained to compete at agility, obedience and working trials. Finnish Lapphunds are also used in Finland as trained tracking dogs for search and rescue and for searching out injured reindeer and elk, unfortunate casualties of the motorways in Finland. There are a number of Finnish Lapphund obedience champions in Finland, and in other countries there are dogs competing in a variety of different canine sports/disciplines.

The breed of course was primarily a herding dog, and this ability has not been forgotten. In Finland it is possible to participate in working tests, where the dogs' aptitude for working with reindeer is examined. While reindeer tests are not easy to arrange outside Finland, I know of Lapphunds in both America and the UK who have received varying levels of herding training with sheep.

As with many intelligent breeds of dog, it is important to point out that a good dog is made, not born. A dog with intelligence combined with a touch of independence will be just as clever in learning bad tricks as good ones, and it is up to the owner to ensure that the training and development of his dog is suitable for the breed. One can never start training a Lapphund too early, and socialisation is very important or else you will soon have a robust adolescent on your hands who has not learned any manners or social skills. A bored dog will be a destructive and unruly dog, so take care to ensure that your dog is well motivated and enjoys a full and varied life. Then you will be justly rewarded with a very honest and loyal companion.

The Lapphund's fabulous

Characteristics

A shining example of versatility and trainability in competition, and of a wonderful companion, is show and obedience champion Kettuharjun Elle, with proud owner Rauno Nisula.

friendly nature has been put to good use, with a number of the breed being temperament-tested and certified to visit hospitals, hospices and retirements homes as therapy dogs.

While the breed is undoubtedly trainable, it definitely does have an independent streak, some more than others. Although most Lapphunds can be let off the lead for free exercise, many are not adverse to a short hunting spree, chasing rabbits and squirrels and anything else that moves, only returning to their owners when the sport has gone to ground! Often the crafty Lapphund first weighs up the pros and cons of such an escapade, making a calculated judgement on the basis of what rewards are on offer.

This independent streak is perhaps more obvious in dogs that are not trained from an early age—the breed can be independent and will soon learn to please itself if not given the incentive to work as part of a team with its human companions. It is interesting that many say the Lapphund has very cat-like characteristics, from its fastidiousness about cleaning itself to an independent attitude that can be very challenging at times.

The question most commonly asked about the breed's characteristics is, 'Does the Lapphund bark?' Certainly the breed can be quick to learn to use its bark to get attention from its owner, and some will bark when very excited, but in most cases the breed is easily taught to be silent. Generally, this is not a noisy breed.

The general good nature of the breed means it fits well as a family dog, enjoying the company of children, other dogs and even cats. Those not socialised with cats at an early age, however, have been known to view the neighbour's cat as a substitute squirrel and therefore good for the chase.

As a herding breed, the Lapphund possesses strong herding instincts, and unless trained specifically to ignore livestock, he should not be trusted loose where farm animals or deer are grazing. The Lapphund's instinct to herd would just be too much for him to bear. In the UK, for example, the farmer has the right to shoot on sight any dog 'worrying' his livestock. For your pet's sake, it is better to take care in these situations and restrict your dog to on-lead exercise.

Another strong trait displayed by Finnish Lapphunds is a definite tendency to dig. I think it is the natural hunter/forager in them that makes them seek out any tasty morsel. In the cold in Finland, they dig holes in the snow and burrow under it, making deep dens that then protect them from the cold and wind. These two factors combine to give the breed a strong inclination to redesign the lawn.

The breed's temperament can be summarised in the points detailed in the translated Finnish standard: 'Keen, courageous, calm and willing to learn. Friendly and faithful.'

PHYSICAL CHARACTERISTICS

Head
The Finnish Lapphund's head is very typical of the spitz-type breeds, being broad and strong with a strong straight muzzle. While the muzzle does taper slightly, there should be no tendency to snipiness. The effect should be a soft and intelligent head, with no sharpness in look or character implied. When viewed from the side, the skull should be slightly domed and the zygomatic arch should be clearly visible, giving a sense of fullness about the cheeks. The muzzle should be slightly shorter than the length of the skull and the two should be separated by a well-pronounced stop. The skull should also be slightly longer than wide.

The breed standard does call for the nose preferably to be black, but it should be remembered that

Characteristics

Head study of young male Rävrackans Mickel Noears.

Stop of head, illustrated by bitch Finch Jahkkas Cariosa.

in a breed with as wide a variety of colours as the Lapphund, the nose itself will be coloured to harmonise with the coat colour. For example, in brown/liver-coloured dogs, the nose will be liver-coloured. The lips of the mouth should be tight and well pigmented.

While the actual shape and proportion of the heads in males and females should be the same, it is important that there are definite differences between the heads of the sexes. The bitch's head should be more refined, with the overall expression of the bitch being more meek or biddable.

The Finnish Lapphund's head should be strong and more teddy-bear like in appearance than that of some of the finely chiselled spitz heads, giving an impression of a calm, humble, primitive servant and not that of the happy smile seen with the more familiar Samoyed.

Eyes

The Lapphund's eyes contribute greatly to the soft and friendly expression. They are oval in shape, clear and bright, with forward vision. The standard asks for a dark brown eye but again, in paler coloured dogs such as the browns, the expectation would be for a paler eye colour. While the Lapphund is a herding dog, one does not hear of the Lapphund's eye being described as an 'eye of control' as with the Border Collie. A difference in the style of working and overall purpose possibly means that the harder eye is not required in this breed, and the darker eye leads to the softer expression.

Mouth

The Finnish Lapphund is required to have a full set of strong white teeth, which should be set in a scissors bite; that is, the upper teeth closely overlapping the teeth in the lower jaw. Care should be taken to avoid breeding specimens with level bites, which is a tendency in some breeds where a shorter muzzle is desired. Missing premolars can also become an issue if there is inadequate length for the jawbone itself.

As with many other breeds, an undershot or overshot mouth in an

Head study of Finnish Lapphund in a very unusual colour.

adult dog must be considered a fault. Of course this in itself may not affect the dog's ability to work as a herding dog, but the extent to which it is malformed could impact on the dog's ability to feed himself; therefore, breeding from animals with poorly formed mouths is very much advised against.

One point to note is that the upper and lower jawbones do develop at different rates. It is not uncommon for a puppy with a nice short muzzle at eight weeks of age to appear to have a level bite, but, as the upper jaw continues to develop, the puppy may then develop a correct scissors bite after a further few weeks. However, of course by the time the adult teeth have appeared at five to six months of age, do not expect there to be dramatic changes in the jawbone development, meaning that a level bite at this stage is unlikely to correct itself.

EARS
The ears of the breed are important to its expression; incorrect ears will result in an untypical expression. As a breed, there can be quite a variation in ear size and ear set. The ears should be small to medium in size and set wide apart on the broad skull. They are triangular in shape with a broad base and can be carried erect (pricked) or semi-erect (tipped).

Standards vary from country to country; an example is the discrepancy here between the standard issued by the breed's homeland, which is the standard recognised by the FCI, and the standard issued by The Kennel Club of England. In the UK, the standard requires that the ears be pricked only, which conflicts with the requirements of the country of origin. It is hoped that the breed club in the UK will be able to approach The Kennel Club with a view to changing this aspect of the standard, but until such a time, the judges in the UK will continue to penalise dogs with semi-erect ears. Quite ironic, when many Finnish champions do in fact have tipped ears.

The standard also asks for the ears to be mobile, and the Lapphund uses it ears to express itself. An alert, keen dog will show its ears high and facing forward, as is often seen in the show ring when a toy or food attracts the dog.

Finnish Lapphund without pricked ears.

THE LAPPHUND'S MEOW

The only perhaps unusual trait of the breed is its definite cat-like tendencies. Lapphunds have a very good sense of balance and can walk along narrow edges and jump from a standing start. They also have a habit of lying down in an odd way, lowering the front legs first and then stretching their back legs out behind them, especially as youngsters, just like a cat. Their attention to cleanliness, washing their paws and then using their paws to wash the face, and also appearing to chew between the pads of the feet and the nails to keep them clean, are all fascinating feline behaviours that the Lapphund exhibits.

When the dog is listening intently, the ears turn back, enabling a wider range of sounds to be picked up; when being meek or coy, the ears turn down and alongside the head so as to be far less conspicuous, softening the expression ever further.

Ears that are too big or too closely set change the expression, and ears that touch one another would not be correct. While tipped ears are equally correct, along with pricked ears, heavy spaniel-like ears should not be accepted. The ears themselves are well furnished with hair inside, and this no doubt offers protection in the Lapphund's original working conditions, where the dogs were exposed to considerable rain and snow. In some cases, the hair inside the ear is quite long and curly, and often in a contrasting colour to the main coat colour of the dog, adding to the overall attractiveness of the ears.

NECK

The Lapphund should have a neck of medium length that is strong and muscular—heavier in males than in females. A good neck is necessary for any breed that is reliant on keeping sight of its quarry in rough conditions. Imagine how a Lapphund would be hindered if it were unable to see the reindeer when moving through thick snow. For this reason, too, you would expect the neck to be well muscled and able to demon-

Characteristics

strate good flexibility of movement both in the neck and head area.

One feature by which I have often been amazed is the Lapphund's apparent ability to turn its head almost through 360°—as an owl can. Maybe this is a strength that goes back to the breed's hunting days, when any advantage in spotting its prey would have given it advantages in the survival stakes in hard winters.

Forequarters

As is expected in a working breed that is required to move easily and with a turn of speed, covering significant distance, a well-laid-back shoulder with good angulation is a necessity. This ensures that the dog can move effortlessly, without too much shock being placed on the front legs.

The upper arm and shoulder blade should be of fairly equal proportions and the angle should be 'open' according to the standard. The author understands this to mean that the angle is better to approach 90° than to be steep, approaching 180°, as too steep an angle will not give the correct reach of front movement.

The elbows themselves should lie slightly lower than the edge of the rib cage. This adds to the flexibility of movement needed in a breed that must be able to change directions on the move at a whim, simply to keep control of an unpredictable herd of reindeer.

Note the breadth between the ears of this brown tricoloured bitch, Finnish Ch Lecibsin Hempukka.

The bones of the legs should be strong and straight and should be parallel when viewed from the front. The pasterns of the Finnish Lapphund, like shock absorbers, are medium in length and set slightly obliquely to the foot to give spring. Flat pasterns would not be suitable for moving across rough terrain in heavy snow.

Body

The back should be firm and strong with a level topline. A weak topline would not be indicative of a dog built to work and be able to cover ground without tiring. The withers themselves should be very muscular and broad, being the powerhouse of the breed (more noticeable in males). This does not mean that the rest of the body should be heavy and coarse. The chest is deep and long, reaching back to the elbows, to give suitable heart and lung room for a working dog, but it is not overly broad, as a thick-set dog is not desirable.

A moderate tuck-up is expected, more defined in the male than in the female. The loin is short and muscular, and the croup is moderate with only a slight slope away to the tail. Overall, the breed should be slightly longer than tall at the withers, with the depth of the body being just less than half of the height at the point of the withers. It is noted that the Paimensukuinen line has a tendency to be longer, more akin to the dimensions of the Border Collie. The Finnish Lapphund should not be square in proportions.

Hindquarters
The hindquarters should give the impression of strength; they should be straight when viewed from behind and parallel, without any tendency to cowhocks or bowed hocks. The breed is only moderately angulated, sufficient to allow freedom of movement when running at speed. Angulation is important for any herding dog, and too little angulation will result in a short-stepped trot, which is a bad fault in the breed. Nonetheless, you would expect the Finnish Lapphund to have more moderate angulation than the Lapponian Herder.

The upper thighs are of medium length, broad and well muscled, as you would expect in a working dog. The angulation comes from the length of the tibia, with the second thigh being long and the hocks being of medium length, so that the angulation is clearly defined but not strong. In the original Finnish and English standards, hind dewclaws were permitted, but these are now indicated under the FCI standard as being undesirable. Many Lapphunds do, however, have hind dewclaws (which are rarely removed in Finland), though they are often quite small and hidden by the extensive feathering on the legs.

Feet
The feet of the Finnish Lapphund should be oval in

Mature cream-coloured male.

shape and well arched with well-sprung pads, not long and flat like those of the Samoyed. The feet should be covered in thick hair to afford protection from the extreme weather. It is interesting to note the apparent opposite requirements of the foot shape between the Samoyed and the Lapphund. The feet of the Samoyed are likened to snowshoes to enable them to move with ease across the snow. Yet you would hardly expect the Lapphund to be designed to suffer at the expense of the extreme weather seen in Lapland, so maybe it is the speed and lightness of feet that help the Lapphund to move over snow without difficulties. Plus, at the same time, the feet are suitably designed for movement across other terrains not encumbered by thick snow, which is important as the Lapphund does not live and work only in the deep snow.

Puppy exhibiting cream colour.

COLOUR

One of the major features of this breed is the sheer diversity of colour that exists. The standard states that all colours are permitted, but that there must be a basic dominant colour, with colours other than the main colour occurring on the head, neck, chest, underside of the body, legs and tail. This means that solid colours are permitted from cream through to black, with bicolours being common, especially black and tan (probably the most common colour seen in Finland) and brown and tan, with or without white markings, forming the tricolour pattern. Another acceptable colour for the show ring is sable.

One very interesting point about the colour is how much puppies can change from their puppy colour to adulthood. Some dogs darken as they get older and some lighten. In some, the tan points fade to cream; in others, sable hairs become more apparent. It is certainly not an easy breed in which to accurately define the colour in an eight-week-old puppy.

The FCI and UK standards do not consider parti- or broken colours to be acceptable, yet in the Paimensukuinen lines such colours as saddle pattern and brindle are relatively common and acceptable to their club.

Colour is not an important factor in the breed and it would

46 FINNISH LAPPHUND

Wolf sable/game colour, exhibited by Lumiturpa Pihla.

Adult Lapphund, exhibiting red coat colour.

Characteristics

be unwise to breed simply for colour, since this would obviously restrict the gene pool available to a breeder. Likewise, judges should not penalise an exhibit purely on the basis of colour, unless of course the colour does not comply with the breed standard. Certainly none of the acceptable colours is considered more correct than another in Finland. The importance of colour will only relate to personal preference with the Finnish Lapphund; however, colour may influence the ability to use the dog in its work, herding reindeer. A light-coloured dog may not be as visible in snow, and a dark dog may not be as easily seen in dim forests.

A Look at Colour Genetics in the Breed

With colour being very varied in the breed, people are interested to know how the colours are inherited. Space (and a limited understanding of the genetics of colour) does not permit me to explain all possibilities here, but I will hopefully give a little insight into some of the factors involved. Note that there are many other factors that influence the pigments, which will result in pattern changes and subtleties of colour that I will not attempt to detail here. Also note that each animal must have a pair of genes, so while in the following I have not shown all of the paired combinations, it is relatively easy

Bear brown bitch with spectacles. Notice the developing spectacles on the puppy.

> **A RAINBOW OF CHOICES**
> Few breeds are as colourful as the Lapphund! All colours are of equal merit, providing that there is a main colour. Acceptable colours include cream, black, red, brown, black and tan or brown and tan with or without white, plus sables.

to see how, with certain pair combinations, a dog itself may be one colour but may produce pups of another colour simply because it carries a recessive colour gene.

The **A series (Agouti)**. The genes in descending order of dominance are:

A^y—dominant yellow or sable. This gives us various types of red and sable (sable being where black guard hairs are apparent, often on the neck, along the spine and the tail);

a^w—wolf sable or grizzle. This is produced by a wide distribution of the agouti hairs. This is a colour common to Scandinavian breeds, when compared to other breeds, perhaps due to the influence of the original agouti wolf pattern;

a^s—saddle. This is characterised by the black saddle markings, often seen on tan. Interestingly this colour is not considered acceptable under the FCI standard as there is no main colour, but many individuals of this type can be seen, especially in *Paimensukuinen linja*/working lines;

a^t—black and tan (in Finland this is called *musta vaalein merkein*, translating as 'black with light marks'). This is the colour pattern commonly occurring in the Finnish Lapphund, with the typical tan points on the legs, the face and above the eyes. (It is possible that some saddle patterns seen in the breed may simply be due to modifications to the black and tan patterns produced by this gene.);

a—recessive black. It is always difficult to ascertain if black dogs are produced as a result of this gene, or if in fact they are really black and tans with very little tan. Solid blacks are seen in the breed and, while the method of inheritance either via **a** or **a^t** is not clear, it would be unlikely that they were the result of the dominant black gene **(A)** simply from the fact that the incidence of this colour is low, and they do not breed true.

The **B (Brown) series** consists of **B** (black) and **b** (brown); in Finland, the latter is called *parkki* and translates as 'bark colour.' This is a simpler series, in which any dog that has black pigment (nose, lips, coat, etc.) must at least have one **B** gene; to show as a brown dog, though, the pairing must be **bb**. It is important with the Lapphund to ensure that names for the colours are not given incorrectly—dogs showing the **bb** gene will be brown and not red (see Agouti series for red).

Characteristics

Left: Black and tan. Right: Brown and tan.

Left: Black and white. Right: Wolf sable puppy.

Left: Smoky grey; notice the shading of the coat. Right: A very unusual colour!

The **C (Colour) series**:

C—colour factor. The pairing **CC** will occur where a dog displays a rich deep tan;

C^e—not fully defined, may have a lightening effect;

c^{ch}—often referred to as Chinchilla and lightens yellow pigment to cream or fawn.

The combinations of these genes will produce a wide variation in the intensity of the tan markings. They also affect the intensity of the brown colour in the **B** series (but not black), so one may find dogs of differing shades of brown or red.

The **E (Extension) series:**

E^m—black mask;

E—no black mask. This gene will be present for all of the dogs that show a normal black or brown or sable colour;

E^{br}—brindle. This colour does exist in Lapphunds, but does not conform to the breed standard's requirement that the main colour must dominate, so is not successful in the show rings in Finland;

e—conversion/fading of black coat to yellow. If **ee** is present, then the colour changes from black or brown to a paler red with no sabling; the added effect of the colour **(C)** series can pale the colour right down to a cream.

Another interesting colour feature, which I have not yet mentioned, is the spectacles, which are unusual markings sometimes seen in this breed. It occurs where there is a lightening in the hair colour immediately around the eyes, giving the appearance of the dog's wearing glasses! This is very striking on an otherwise black or dark brown dog.

Since this feature is not common in the breeds where colour inheritance has been well documented, it is difficult to comment on how this may be inherited. It could possibly be due to a modification in the black and tan series, bringing about a different pattern to the more common marks above the eyes, or perhaps it is affected by another gene series or modifier. Looking through the other spitz breeds, no similar markings are seen. The Keeshond standard requires 'well defined spectacles,' but these spectacles are formed as fine-pencilled black lines around the eye, whereas those seen in the Finnish Lapphund are areas of paler hair around the eyes. In the Norwegian Elkhound, spectacles are undesirable!

With such a variety of coat colour, one also needs to note that other pigments will vary and that not all Lapphunds will have black noses. Brown dogs would, of course, be expected to have liver-coloured noses; where the 'paling' genes are present, it may well be that these dogs will show lighter pigment in nose leather colour, lips and eye colour. 'Snow-nose' is also commonly seen in the breed,

Characteristics 51

Brown or *parkki* colour.

Sable colour.

FINNISH LAPPHUND

Spectacles in the Keeshond, shown here, appear as 'pencilled' lines around the eyes, differing from the spectacles seen in the Finnish Lapphund.

Finnish Lapphund with clearly defined spectacles of lighter hair around eyes.

especially in winter, where the normal dark nose pales to show a paler stripe down the centre. However, like in the Alaskan Malamute, I have seen young Lapphund puppies that were born during the summer show this strange nose colouring, even when their coat colour is the deepest black, so it may be affected by factors other than sunlight in this breed. Certainly in Finland the snow-nose is not considered a fault in the Lapphund.

TAIL

It is interesting and perhaps amusing to note that it is the extremities of this breed that prompt much debate and discussion. The ears and tail of the Finnish Lapphund are very important to the dog's total appearance and attitude, and perhaps are the key features differentiating the Lapphund from many of the other spitz breeds.

The spitz-type breeds span many of the groups as defined by national breed clubs like The Kennel Club and the American Kennel Club, appearing in perhaps half of the groups. While breeds like the Finnish Spitz, Pomeranian, Japanese Shiba, Akita, Keeshond and Samoyed are all classified as spitz types, they all have different tail carriages. Judges, exhibitors and breeders always must be aware that what is correct for one spitz breed may not be correct for the next.

To illustrate, the Finnish Spitz requires a plumed tail that curves in a circle so that the tip touches the thigh; it is held quite tight to the body. The Pomeranian has a high-set tail turned over the back and carried on the back. The Akita has a large high-set tail carried over the back in a curl (from a three-quarter to a double curl). The Akita's tail is required to dip to or below the back and, where the tail is only a three-quarter curl, the tip should reach to the flank. Sickle or uncurled tails are not acceptable.

Characteristics

The Keeshond has a high-set tail, tightly curled; in fact, a double curl is much sought after and the tail must be carried tight at all times.

The purpose of these tail carriage descriptions is to show that each breed is quite different, and so it is with the Finnish Lapphund as well. The tail should be set rather high, being medium in length and covered in profuse long hair. The tip of the tail may have a J-formed hook (which is not permitted in some spitz breeds). The crucial point to note is that when the dog is moving, the tail is curled over the back or the side; in repose, it may hang.

This latter point is not emphasised in the English version of the standard, and many judges do in fact penalise dogs that let their tails drop when standing. However, this is in fact a feature of the breed, and constant high tail carriage should not be required. While the translated version of the Finnish standard implies a 'rather high' tail set, it should be remembered that the Lapphund does have a slight slope to the croup. Thus, the tail will not be as high-set as many of the other spitz breed and it is this fact that enables the Lapphund to use a wide range of tail carriages.

The Lapphund should be able to express itself with its tail. In a wild state, a dog will use its tail to give signals to other dogs, obvious means of communication for the dog to the fellow pack animals, both canine and human. The dog's ability to relax the tail also means that in severe weather conditions the tail can be used to wrap about the body, helping to insulate the dog from its sub-zero surroundings. When you see a Lapphund tightly curled with its head tucked into its tail, you can see that warm air expelled from its nose is in fact being conserved, This, with the thick insulation of the coat, helps the dog keep warm while buried in snow holes.

GAIT/MOVEMENT

The standard requires an effortless gait, which can change with ease from a trot to a gallop, the latter being the most natural style of movement for the breed. When at work, the dog should be agile, fast and able to move to cover wander-

A Finnish Lapphund *can* drop its tail when standing.

FINNISH LAPPHUND

The breed's magnificent plumed tail, exhibited by Int Danish Ch Fidelis Uuriel.

ing reindeer. When running free, the Lapphund tends to gallop rather than trot, unlike the breed's close cousin, the Lapponian Herder, which favours the fast trot as its chosen working pace.

As with many of the herding breeds, the action on the move is perceived to be parallel, but, as the pace of the trot speeds up, there will be a tendency for the legs to converge. However, this is not something that would be readily seen if the Lapphund were moving naturally, as no doubt the dog would change from a steady trot to a gallop and not demonstrate a fast trot. In the show ring, judges often think that fast movement equates to soundness, but with a breed built to gallop, one should not expect to see a fast-gaiting trot like that of the Border Collie or German Shepherd. As detailed above, as the dog moves, the tail would be expected to rise over or on the side of the back.

COAT

The Finnish Lapphund is a profusely coated breed. The outer coat should be long, straight and very harsh, whereas the undercoat is soft and dense to provide adequate insulation from the harsh winters. This type of coat is often called a double coat. The coat on the head and the front of the legs is shorter. In males, a noticeable mane should be present, which often extends up to the root of the ears, making the ears almost invisible.

The harshness of the coat means that the coat requires little maintenance as it is not inclined to mat or knot. Special care is mainly required on the longer feathering around the ears, mane and legs, especially the heavier feathering on the hind legs that create the trousers or 'knickers.'

By having a harsh straight outer coat, the Finnish Lapphund is in effect fairly waterproof, the rain and snow easily dripping off. A soft curly coat would trap the rain and snow, and the dog would become too cold. Obviously, as a long-coated breed, the Lapphund will shed coat (moult) and the frequency of this will depend on a number of factors. Dogs kept in centrally heated conditions will no doubt lose hair more frequently than those living outside and needing their coats to keep warm.

In the UK, US and other countries with similar changes in season, the dogs do tend to moult in the autumn, as if they are preparing for the winter, shedding any dead hair and growing fresh new hair for the winter. Unspayed bitches may moult up to twice a year as hormonal influences associated with heat cycles can prompt a moult. Certainly, as with many other breeds, the bitches shed tremendous amounts of coat 8–12 weeks after whelping their litters, losing so much hair that they can resemble Lapponian Herders more than Lapphunds!

HEIGHT AND WEIGHT

The ideal height for a male is 49 cms (19 ins) with breed tolerance of 3 cms (about 1 in) in either direction, providing for a range of 46–52 cms (18–20.5 ins). For bitches, the ideal height is given as 44 cms (17 ins), with the range being 41–47 cms (16–18.5 ins). Nonetheless, the standard states that breed type is more important than the size.

Weight is more difficult to give a 'normal range,' but 15–24 kgs (33–53 lbs) would not be unreasonable (weight, of course, should be in proportion to height). The Lapphund has a healthy appetite and care should be taken not to let the breed become overweight, as a fat dog is not a healthy dog, and certainly it would not be able to work tirelessly if carrying excess weight.

FAULTS

The translated standard from the Finnish Kennel Club gives a list of faults, though these are not included in The Kennel Club standard:
- Males not masculine, and females not feminine;
- Light head;
- Insufficient stop;
- Drop ears;
- Tail carriage continuously lower than topline;
- Over-angulated or too straight rear angulation;
- Lack of undercoat;
- Flat coat;
- Curly outer coat;
- Basic colour indistinct.

Under the Finnish system, the following faults are deemed to be eliminating faults:
- Overshot or undershot mouth;
- Kinky tail.

Mature rough-coated male, Finnish Ch Kiedalas Cerrih.

BREED STANDARD FOR THE
FINNISH LAPPHUND

A breed standard represents a 'blueprint' for a given breed and gives guidelines on the conformation and general characteristics of the breed for which it was written. Over the years (since 1945), since the first standard was written for the Finnish Lapphund, it has been revised and 'fine-tuned' by the Finnish Kennel Club in conjunction with the breed club in Finland to produce the latest revision, which was approved in March 1999.

The standard sets out to clearly define the breed features that make the Finnish Lapphund what it is and set it apart from other breeds. The standard is used by breeders and judges alike to identify good and bad breed points in individual dogs. Since the perfect dog has yet to be born, no individual dog will conform wholly and perfectly to everyone's interpretation of the breed standard. Yet the breed standard of the Finnish Lapphund should, on the whole, enable breeders to work toward a

Just a fraction of the Finnish Lapphund rainbow of colours on display at a dog show.

uniform type and enable judges to assess this type in conformation classes.

The breed standard for the UK is not the same as the FCI standard used in other European countries, and it does not fully take account of the 1999 revised Finnish standard. The main differences include the omission in the English standard of the acceptance of tipped ears, and the fact that the English standard does not mention that the tail may hang when the dog is standing at rest. The UK standard also does not highlight those features that are considered to be notable faults.

As with any breed, it is important to view the Finnish Lapphund as a whole dog, and the essence of the breed is made up of all of the points; no one feature of the breed should be exaggerated. The general type as defined in the standard must always be viewed with the breed's purpose in mind, a working reindeer-herding dog. If the breed's purpose becomes forgotten and the breed type becomes exaggerated in any way, then the true Finnish Lapphund will be lost.

THE FCI BREED STANDARD FOR THE FINNISH LAPPHUND (SUOMENLAPINKOIRA)

ORIGIN
Finland.

Finnish Ch Staalon Lapintähti.

DATE OF PUBLICATION OF THE ORIGINAL VALID STANDARD
16.11.1996

UTILIZATION
Originally a herder and watchdog used in work of keeping reindeer. Today also popular as a companion dog.

BREEDER'S BLUEPRINT
If you are considering breeding your bitch, it is very important that you are familiar with the breed standard. Reputable breeders breed with the intention of producing dogs that are as close as possible to the standard and that contribute to the advancement of the breed. Study the standard for both physical appearance and temperament, and make certain your bitch and your chosen stud dog measure up.

FINNISH LAPPHUND

Black and tan dog of correct balance, type and structure in profile.

FCI Classification
Group 5, Section 3.4 (Nordic watchdogs and herders), without working trial.

Brief Historical Summary
For hundreds of years the Lapps have used dogs of the same type as Finnish Lapphund as reindeer herders and watchdogs in Fennoscandia and in the northern parts of Russia. Due to these dogs, the first standard of the Lapponian Herder was established by the Finnish Kennel Club in 1945. The breed's name was changed into Lapphound in 1967. In the 1970s the type and picture of the breed became fixed, the standard has been specified several times. The breed name was again changed into Finnish Lapphund in 1993. The breed type has become stable in a short time and today the breed is very popular mainly as a house and hobby dog in the whole of Finland.

General Appearance
Smaller than medium sized, the conformation is strong for the size, slightly longer than the height at the withers. Long and thick coated dog with pricked ears.

Important Proportions
The depth of the body is slightly less than the half of the height at the withers. The muzzle is slightly shorter than the skull. The skull is slightly longer than broad, the depth is the same as the breadth.

Behaviour and Temperament
Intelligent, courageous, calm and willing to learn. Friendly and faithful.

Head
Strong in outline, rather broad. *Cranial Region:* Broad, the skull is slightly convex. The forehead is rather domed. The frontal furrow is clearly defined. *Stop:* Clearly defined.

Facial Region
Nose: Preferably black, yet harmonising with the coat colour. *Muzzle:* Strong, broad and straight; viewed from above and in profile evenly, but only slightly

tapering. *Lips*: Tight. *Jaws/Bite*: The jaws are strong. Scissors bite. *Cheeks*: The zygomatic arches are clearly marked. *Eyes*: Dark brown in colour, yet harmonising with the coat colour, oval shaped. The expression is soft and friendly. *Ears*: Medium sized, carried erect or semi-erect, set rather apart, rather broad at the base, triangular in shape and very mobile.

NECK
Medium in length, strong and covered with profuse hair.

BODY
Withers: Muscular and broad, slightly marked. *Back*: Strong and straight. *Loin*: Short and muscular. *Croup*: Of medium length, well developed, only slightly oblique. *Chest*: Deep, rather long, reaching almost the elbows, not very broad. The ribs are slightly arched; the forechest clearly visible, not very strong. *Underline*: Slightly tucked up.

TAIL
Set rather high, medium in length, covered with profuse and long hair. The tip of the tail may have a J-formed hook. In movement the tail is curved over the back or side, in rest it may hang.

LIMBS
Forequarters: *General Appearance:* Powerful with strong bones. Viewed from the front straight and parallel. *Shoulders*: Slightly oblique. *Upper Arms*: As long as the shoulder blades. The angle between shoulder and upper arm is rather open. *Elbows*: Placed slightly lower than the lower edge of the rib cage, pointing straight backwards. *Forearms*: Rather strong, vertical. *Carpus*: Flexible. *Pasterns*: Of medium length, slightly oblique. *Feet*: Rather high, oval rather than round, covered with dense hair. The pads are elastic with the sides covered with dense hair.
Hindquarters: *General Appearance*: Strong boned, powerful, viewed from behind straight and parallel. The angulation is clearly marked but not very strong. *Upper Thigh*: Of medium length, rather broad with well developed muscles. *Stifle*: Pointed forward, the angulation is rather clearly marked. *Second Thigh:* Relatively long and sinewy.

Head study, showing correct type and proportion.

FINNISH LAPPHUND

All features of the head contribute to the overall soft, friendly, intelligent expression, implying no sharpness.

Judge Juliette Cunliffe, examining a Finnish Lapphund. Judging is a 'hands-on' procedure as the judge feels for correct bone structure.

Hocks: Moderately low, the angulation is clearly marked but not very strong. *Metatarsus*: Rather short, strong and vertical. *Feet*: As front feet. Dewclaws are not desirable.

GAIT
Effortless. Changes easily from trot to gallop, which is the most natural style of movement. The legs move parallel. When working agile and fast.

SKIN
Tight overall without wrinkles.

COAT
Hair: Profuse, especially the males have an abundant mane. The outer coat is long, straight and harsh. On the head and on the front side of the legs, the coat is shorter. There has to be an undercoat that is soft and dense.
Colour: All colours are permitted. The basic colour must be dominant. Colours other than the basic colour can occur on head, neck, chest, underside of the body, legs and tail.

SIZE
Height at the Withers: Ideal height: males 49 cms and females 44 cms with a tolerance of 3 cms. The type is more important than the size.

FAULTS
Any departure from the foregoing points should be considered a fault and the seriousness with which the fault should be regarded should be in exact proportion to its degree.
- Males not masculine and females not feminine

Breed Standard

The outline shows the correct body structure underneath the coat.

Faults: Short neck; upright shoulders; weak pasterns and flat feet; narrow and cowhocked in rear.

Faults: Short neck; long back; low on leg.

Faults: Narrow pinched front; upright shoulders; toes out; high in rear; lacking angulation behind; generally lacking substance.

Breed judging in Finland at a Championship Show.

FINNISH LAPPHUND

- Light head
- Insufficient stop
- Drop-ears
- Over angulated or too straight rear angulation
- Tail carriage continuously lower than the topline
- Lack of undercoat
- Flat coat
- Curly outer coat
- Basic colour indistinct

DISQUALIFYING FAULTS
- Overshot or undershot mouth
- Kinky tail

NOTE
Male animals should have two apparently normal testicles fully descended into the scrotum.

Correct structure is necessary for correct movement, which is evaluated in the show ring. The Finnish Lapphund's gait should appear effortless, and the gallop is the breed's chosen gait for working purposes.

YOUR PUPPY
FINNISH LAPPHUND

HOW TO SELECT A PUPPY
As with many other irresistible breeds, the Finnish Lapphund puppy is absolutely gorgeous, resembling a very fluffy, chunky teddy bear, and it would be easy for anyone to fall head over heels in love with one. So for anyone contemplating the breed, make sure that you visit and get to know the adults first before going to look at the fluffy puppies, just to make sure that the adult members of the breed represent the right dog for you. Remember that any dog is an adult for much, much longer than he is a pup!

The first step in selecting a puppy is to decide which type of Finnish Lapphund suits you and then to find a breeder of this type. You need to decide whether you favour the Finnish Lapphund type as defined in the standard, or the sub-type—the Paimensukuinen type—and then to approach the appropriate breeders. Finnish Lapphund breed club members operate under a Code of Ethics, which is intended to protect the future health and quality of the breed, so you should acquaint yourself with the Code of Ethics of your country's breed club and make sure that your selected breeder is familiar with it.

An important point of consideration is that all of the breeder's stock, prior to mating, must be eye-tested for hereditary cataracts (HC) and progressive retinal atrophy (PRA) under the appropriate testing scheme, meaning that a current annual eye certificate must be held prior to mating. All stock also should be examined under your country's testing scheme for the

> **PUPPY APPEARANCE**
> Your puppy should have a well-fed appearance but not a distended abdomen, which may indicate worms or incorrect feeding, or both. The body should be firm, with a solid feel. The skin of the abdomen should be pale pink and clean, without signs of scratching or rash.

PREPARING FOR PUP

Unfortunately, when a puppy is bought by someone who does not take into consideration the time and attention that dog ownership requires, it is the puppy who suffers when he is either abandoned or placed in a shelter by a frustrated owner. So all of the 'homework' you do in preparation for your pup's arrival will benefit you both. The more informed you are, the more you will know what to expect and the better equipped you will be to handle the ups and downs of raising a puppy. Hopefully, everyone in the household is willing to do his part in raising and caring for the pup. The anticipation of owning a dog often brings a lot of promises from excited family members: 'I will walk him every day,' 'I will feed him,' 'I will house-train him,' etc., but these things take time and effort, and promises can be forgotten easily once the novelty of the new pet has worn off.

control of hip dysplasia.

Copies of the relevant health certification should be available for you to see. You may also want to ask for a copy of the puppy's pedigree, where any known PRA- and HC-affected animals should be highlighted for you, so that risks associated with these conditions can be identified.

Another factor to consider is that the Finnish Lapphund is a late-maturing breed, so no breeder should breed from any bitch, or allow his dog to be used on any bitch, before she is 18 months of age or in successive seasons, except on the written advice of a vet. Any breeder who does not adhere to that policy is not a reputable breeder and not one from whom you should purchase a puppy.

Whether you hope to work your Lapphund in a chosen canine sport or other hobby may also influence your decision when choosing the breeder of your puppy. Some breeders may be able to demonstrate proven skills and/or titles of the parents and others in the pup's background, which may indicate whether his lines are well suited to or proven to be successful in your choice of pursuit.

Where animals are being selected as family pets, it is generally accepted that puppies reared in the breeder's home will be better socialised than those reared in a kennel environment. This, too, may affect the choice of your puppy's breeder.

Having selected a breeder or two, you should then be prepared to wait patiently for your puppy. The breed is still relatively new to the UK and US, and there are only a limited number of breeding bitches. Therefore, you may have quite a wait before a suitable litter is born.

When you visit the litter, you should already have in mind what characteristics are important to you and how you are going to choose your special pup. Colour may be one aspect that influences you, and, if so, perhaps you will select a breeder whose litter is likely to produce the colours that you find attractive. (With some colours being recessive, you will need to research which lines are more likely to produce the colours of your choice.) Keep in mind, of course, that colour is a minor consideration when choosing a puppy and, in the Finnish Lapphund, it is extremely difficult to predict with any accuracy what colour the adult dog will be based only on the puppy's appearance. Even experienced breeders are surprised by how a puppy's coat colour changes with maturity.

PUPPY SELECTION
Your selection of a good puppy can be determined by your needs. A show potential or a good pet? It is your choice. Every puppy, however, should be of good temperament. Although show-quality puppies are bred and raised with emphasis on physical conformation, responsible breeders strive for equally good temperament. Do not buy from a breeder who concentrates solely on physical beauty at the expense of personality.

When considering the sex of your puppy, there are some factors that might be helpful. As with many breeds, the male Finnish Lapphund is on average taller and heavier than the female; males also have noticeably more coat, especially

FINNISH LAPPHUND

Cantavia Siinipika, a lovely blue female puppy.

around the neck, to produce a definite mane. Females are more biddable than males and perhaps therefore more easily trained for the less experienced owner.

By watching the whole litter at rest and play over a period of time, and with the breeder's advice, you will be able to identify the more dominant puppies and get some idea of each pup's individual characteristics. You may wish to have neither the most dominant, or alpha, pup in the litter nor the least outgoing tyke. Always seek the advice of the breeder as to which of the pups might best suit you and your family.

If you are planning on showing (or breeding), conformation will be important to you. Therefore, you should examine the structure of each pup and relate it to the points detailed in the breed standard, comparing each puppy to its littermates to see which pup has the shape and structure that best conforms to the standard. Experienced breeders will no doubt be able to identify the pup with the desirable short muzzle and correct length of back. Ideally, at this stage, you would not be looking for a long-nosed pup or one that was too leggy.

I find that coat length and adult colour are more difficult to judge in young pups, as is mature adult size. The smallest pup in the litter may grow on and catch up to his bigger siblings. When you come to make the final selection, you

HEALTH FIRST
You should not even think about buying a puppy that looks sick, undernourished, overly frightened or nervous. Sometimes a timid puppy will warm up to you after a 30-minute 'let's-get-acquainted' session.

should check that your pup has the correct scissors bite, and that, in the case of a male pup, the testicles are fully descended (sometimes this may not be obvious at eight weeks of age and you may need to seek confirmation with a vet).

COMMITMENT OF OWNERSHIP

After considering all of these factors, you have most likely already made some very important decisions about selecting your puppy. You have chosen the Finnish Lapphund, which means that you have decided which characteristics you want in a dog, which type of Lapphund you desire and what kind of dog will best fit into your family and lifestyle. If you have selected a breeder, you have gone a step further—you have done your research and found a responsible, conscientious person who breeds quality Finnish Lapphunds and who should become a reliable source of help as you and your puppy adjust to life together. If you have observed a litter in action, you have obtained a firsthand look at the dynamics of a puppy 'pack' and, thus, you have learned about each pup's individual personality—perhaps you have even found one that particularly appeals to you.

However, even if you have not yet found the Finnish Lapphund puppy of your dreams, observing pups will help you learn to recognise certain behaviour and to determine what a pup's behaviour indicates about his temperament. You will be able to pick out which pups are the leaders, which ones are less outgoing, which ones are confident, shy, playful, friendly, aggressive, etc. Equally as important, you will learn to recognise what a healthy pup should look and act like. All of these things will help you in your search, and when you find the Finnish Lapphund that was meant for you, you will know it!

Researching your breed,

Chelville Eija grew up to become a Finnish champion.

DOCUMENTATION

Two important documents you will get from the breeder are the pup's pedigree and registration certificate. The breeder should register the litter and each pup with a breed registry or kennel club, and it is necessary for you to have the paperwork if you plan on showing or breeding in the future.

Make sure you know the breeder's intentions on which type of registration he will obtain for the pup. There are limited registrations that may prohibit the dog from being shown or bred, or from competing in non-conformation trials such as obedience or agility if the breeder feels that the pup is not of sufficient quality to do so. There is also a type of registration that will permit the dog in non-conformation competition only.

On the reverse side of the registration certificate, the new owner may find the transfer section, which must be signed by the breeder.

selecting a responsible breeder and observing adults and pups are all important steps on the way to dog ownership. You cannot be too careful when it comes to deciding on the type of dog you want and finding out about your prospective pup's background. Buying a puppy is not—or *should* not be—just another whimsical purchase. This is one instance in which you actually do get to choose your own family!

You may be thinking that buying a puppy should be fun—it should not be so serious and so much work. Keep in mind that your puppy is not a cuddly stuffed toy or decorative lawn ornament; rather, he is a living creature that will become a real member of your family. You will come to realise that, while buying a puppy is a pleasurable and exciting endeavour, it is not something to be taken lightly. Relax…the fun will start when the pup comes home!

Always keep in mind that a puppy is nothing more than a baby in a furry disguise…a baby who is virtually helpless in a human world and who trusts his owner for fulfilment of his basic needs for survival. In addition to food, water and shelter, your pup needs care, protection, guidance and love. If you are not prepared to commit to this, then you are not prepared to own a dog.

'Wait a minute,' you say. 'How hard could this be? All of my neighbours own dogs and they seem to be doing just fine. Why should I have to worry about all of this?' Well, you should not worry about it; in fact, you will probably find that once your Finnish Lapphund pup gets used to his new home, he will fall into his place in the family quite naturally. However, it never hurts to emphasise the commitment of dog ownership. With some time and patience, it is really not too difficult to raise a curious and exuberant Finnish Lapphund pup to be a well-adjusted and well-mannered adult dog—a dog that could be your most loyal friend.

PREPARING PUPPY'S PLACE IN YOUR HOME

Researching your breed and finding a breeder are only two aspects of the 'homework' you will have to do before taking your Finnish Lapphund puppy home. You will also have to prepare your home and family for the new addition. Much as you would prepare a nursery for a newborn baby, you will need to designate a place in your home that will be the puppy's own. How you prepare your home will depend on how much freedom the dog will be allowed. Whatever you decide, you must ensure that he has a place that he can 'call his own.'

ARE YOU A FIT OWNER?
If the breeder from whom you are buying a puppy asks you a lot of personal questions, do not be insulted. Such a breeder wants to be sure that you will be a fit provider for his puppy.

When you take your new puppy into your home, you are bringing him into what will become his home as well. Obviously, you did not buy a puppy with the intentions of catering to his every whim and allowing him to 'rule the roost,' but in order for a puppy to grow into a stable, well-adjusted dog, he has to feel comfortable in his surroundings. Remember, he is leaving the warmth and security of his mother and littermates, as

Your Finnish Lapphund will appreciate a comfortable place of his own throughout his life.

well as the familiarity of the only place he has ever known, so it is important to make his transition as easy as possible. By preparing a place in your home for the puppy, you are making him feel as welcome as possible in a strange new place. It should not take him long to get used to it, but the sudden shock of being transplanted is somewhat traumatic for a young pup. Imagine how a small child would feel in the same situation—that is how your puppy must be feeling. It is up to you to reassure him and to let him know, 'Little Finn, you are going to like it here!'

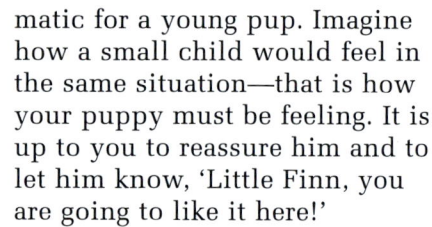

WHAT YOU SHOULD BUY

CRATE

To someone unfamiliar with the use of crates in dog training, it may seem like punishment to shut a dog in a crate, but this is not the case at all. Although all breeders do not advocate crate training, more and more breeders and trainers are recommending crates as preferred tools for pet puppies as well as show puppies.

Crates are not cruel—crates have many humane and highly effective uses in dog care and training. For example, crate training is a popular and very successful house-training method. In addition, a crate can keep your dog safe during travel and, perhaps most importantly, a crate provides your dog with a place of his own in your home. It serves as a 'doggie bedroom' of sorts—your Finnish Lapphund can curl up in his crate when he wants to sleep or when he just needs a break. Many dogs sleep in their crates overnight. With soft bedding and his favourite toy, a crate

> **YOUR SCHEDULE...**
> If you lead an erratic, unpredictable life, with daily or weekly changes in your work requirements, consider the problems of owning a dog. The new puppy has to be fed regularly, socialised (loved, petted, handled, introduced to other people) and, most importantly, allowed to visit outdoors for toilet training. As the dog gets older, it can be more tolerant of deviations in its feeding and toilet relief.

Puppy

TIME TO GO HOME
Breeders rarely release puppies until they are eight to ten weeks of age. This is an acceptable age for most breeds of dog, excepting toy breeds, which are not released until around 12 weeks, given their petite sizes. If a breeder has a puppy that is 12 weeks of age or older, it is likely well socialised and house-trained. Be sure that it is otherwise healthy before deciding to take it home.

protection for the dog.

The size of the crate is another thing to consider. Puppies do not stay puppies forever—in fact, sometimes it seems as if they grow right before your eyes. A small crate may be fine for a very young Finnish Lapphund pup, but it will not do him much good for long! Unless you have the money and the inclination to buy a new becomes a cosy pseudo-den for your dog. Like his ancestors, he too will seek out the comfort and retreat of a den—you just happen to be providing him with something a little more luxurious than what his early ancestors enjoyed.

As far as purchasing a crate, the type that you buy is up to you. It will most likely be one of the two most popular types: wire or fibreglass. There are advantages and disadvantages to each type. For example, a wire crate is more open, allowing the air to flow through and affording the dog a view of what is going on around him, while a fibreglass crate is sturdier. Both can double as travel crates, providing

Your local pet shop should carry a variety of crates. Select a sturdy crate for your Finnish Lapphund puppy that is large enough to accommodate him when he reaches full adult size.

Once acclimated, your Finnish Lapphund will accept his crate as his own private retreat, and you will be able to use the crate to confine him safely indoors and out, wherever you go.

crate every time your pup has a growth spurt, it is better to get one that will accommodate your dog both as a pup and at full size. A medium-size crate will be necessary for a fully-grown Finnish Lapphund, who can stand up to approximately 52 cms (20.5 ins) high, depending on gender and the individual dog.

CRATE-TRAINING TIPS

During crate training, you should partition off the section of the crate in which the pup stays. If he is given too big an area, this will hinder your training efforts. Crate training is based on the fact that a dog does not like to soil his sleeping quarters, so it is ineffective to keep a pup in an area that is so big that he can eliminate in one end and get far enough away from it to sleep. Also, you want to make the crate den-like for the pup. Blankets and a favourite toy will make the crate cosy for the small pup; as he grows, you may want to evict some of his 'roommates' to make more room. It will take some coaxing at first, but be patient. Given some time to get used to it, your pup will adapt to his new home-within-a-home quite nicely.

BEDDING

Soft bedding in the dog's crate will help the dog feel more at home, and you may also like to provide a small blanket. First, this will take the place of the leaves, twigs, etc. that the pup would use in the wild to make a den; the pup can make his own 'burrow' in the crate. Although your pup is far removed from his den-making ancestors, the denning instinct is still a part of his genetic makeup. Second, until you take your pup home, he has been sleeping amid the warmth of his mother and litter-

Puppy

mates, and while a blanket is not the same as a warm, breathing body, it still provides heat and something with which to snuggle. You will want to wash your pup's bedding frequently in case he has a toileting 'accident' in his crate, and replace or remove any padding or blanket that becomes ragged and starts to fall apart.

Toys

Toys are a must for dogs of all ages, especially for curious playful pups. Puppies are the 'children' of the dog world, and what child does not love toys? Chew toys provide enjoyment for both dog and owner—your dog will enjoy playing with his favourite toys, while you will enjoy the fact that they distract him from chewing on your expensive shoes and leather sofa. Puppies love to chew; in fact, chewing is a physical need for pups as they are teething, and everything looks appetising! The full range of your possessions—from old tea towel to Oriental carpet—are fair game in the eyes of a teething pup. Puppies are not all that discerning when it comes to finding something literally to 'sink their teeth into'—everything tastes great!

For its size, the Lapphund has very strong teeth and jaws, and, while the breed is not

TOYS, TOYS, TOYS!

With a big variety of dog toys available, and so many that look like they would be a lot of fun for a dog, be careful in your selection. It is amazing what a set of puppy teeth can do to an innocent-looking toy, so, obviously, safety is a major consideration. Be sure to choose the most durable products that you can find. Hard nylon bones and toys are a safe bet, and many of them are offered in different scents and flavours that will be sure to capture your dog's attention. It is always fun to play a game of catch with your dog, and there are balls and flying discs that are specially made to withstand dog teeth.

Your local pet shop will have a large variety of leads from which you can select one that is suitable for your Finnish Lapphund.

renowned for its destructive behaviour, if bored it will chew. Suitable toys would include large natural bones as purchased from pet suppliers (not small bones left from the family meal) or bone-substitute toys, specifically designed to enable the dog to gnaw on the hard nylon-type surfaces and to facilitate keeping teeth and gums healthy. Other toys include heavy-duty rubber toys. I would recommend purchasing the toy at the larger-size scale for durability rather than those suited for medium-sized dogs, purely because of the strength of jaw of the breed.

Lead

A nylon lead is probably the best option, as it is the most resistant to puppy teeth should your pup take a liking to chewing on his lead. Of course, this is a habit that should be nipped in the bud, but, if your pup likes to chew on his lead, he has a very slim chance of being able to chew through the strong nylon. Nylon leads are also lightweight, which is good for a young Finnish Lapphund who is just getting used to the idea of walking on a lead.

For everyday walking and safety purposes, the nylon lead is a good choice. As your pup grows up and gets used to walking on the lead, and can do it politely, you may want to purchase a flexible lead. These leads allow you to extend the length to give the dog a broader area to explore or to shorten the length to keep the dog near you. Of course, there are leads designed for training purposes, but these are not necessary for routine walks.

Collar

Your pup should get used to wearing a collar all the time since you will want to attach his ID tags to it; plus, you have to attach the lead to something! A lightweight nylon collar is a good choice. Make certain that the collar fits snugly enough so

CHOOSE AN APPROPRIATE COLLAR

The **BUCKLE COLLAR** is the standard collar used for everyday purposes. Be sure that you adjust the buckle on growing puppies. Check it every day. It can become too tight overnight! These collars can be made of leather or nylon. Attach your dog's identification tags to this collar.

The **CHOKE COLLAR** is designed for training. It is constructed of highly polished steel so that it slides easily through the stainless steel loop. The idea is that the dog controls the pressure around his neck and he will stop pulling if the collar becomes uncomfortable. It should *not* be used on heavily coated breeds like the Finnish Lapphund.

The **HALTER** is for a trained dog that has to be restrained to prevent running away, chasing a cat and the like. Considered the most humane of all collars, it is frequently used on smaller dogs on which collars are not comfortable.

FINNISH LAPPHUND

Your local pet shop will have a variety of food and water bowls. Choose durable, easily cleaned bowls for your Finnish Lapphund.

that the pup cannot wriggle out of it, but is loose enough so that it will not be uncomfortably tight around the pup's neck. You should be able to fit a finger between the pup's neck and the collar. It may take some time for your pup to get used to wearing the collar, but soon he will not even notice that it is there. Choke collars are made for training, but are not recommended for use on heavily coated breeds like the Lapphund, as the collar can pull and damage the coat.

FOOD AND WATER BOWLS
Your pup will need two bowls, one for food and one for water. You may want two sets of bowls, one for indoors and one for outdoors, depending on where the dog will be fed and where he will be spending time. Stainless steel or sturdy plastic bowls are popular choices. Plastic bowls are more chewable, but dogs tend not to chew on the steel variety, which can be sterilised. It is important to buy sturdy bowls since anything is in danger of being chewed by puppy teeth and you do not want your dog to be constantly chewing apart his bowl (for his safety and for your purse!).

CLEANING SUPPLIES
Until a pup is house-trained, you will be doing a lot of cleaning. 'Accidents' will occur, which is

acceptable in the beginning stages of toilet training because the puppy does not know any better. All you can do is be prepared to clean up any accidents as soon as they happen. Old towels, paper kitchen towels, newspapers and a safe disinfectant are good to have on hand.

BEYOND THE BASICS
The items previously discussed are the bare necessities. You will find out what else you need as you go along—grooming supplies, flea/tick protection, baby gates to partition a room, etc. These things will vary depending on your situation, but it is important that you have everything you need to feed and make your Finnish Lapphund comfortable in his first few days at home.

Though no dog owner's favourite chore, you should always clean up after your dog has relieved himself. Fortunately, you can purchase tools to aid in the cleanup task.

Food bowl or chew toy...? Nothing is safe from the mouth of a teething pup!

PUPPY-PROOFING YOUR HOME

Aside from making sure that your Finnish Lapphund will be comfortable in your home, you also have to make sure that your home is safe for your Finnish Lapphund. This means taking precautions that your pup will not get into anything he should not get into and that there is nothing within his reach that may harm him should he sniff it, chew it, inspect it, etc. This probably seems obvious since, while you are primarily concerned with your pup's safety, at the same time you do not want your belongings to be ruined. Breakables should be placed out of reach if your dog is to have full run of the house. If he is to be limited to certain places within the house, keep any potentially dangerous items in the 'off-limits' areas.

An electrical lead can pose a danger should the puppy decide to taste it—and who is going to convince a pup that it would not make a great chew toy? Electrical leads should be fastened tightly against the wall and kept from puppy teeth. If your dog is going to spend time in a crate, make sure that there is nothing near his crate that he can reach if he sticks his curious little nose or paws through the openings. Just as you would with a child, keep all household cleaners and

TOXIC PLANTS
Examine your grass and garden landscaping before bringing your puppy home. Many varieties of plants have leaves, stems or flowers that are toxic if ingested, and you can depend on a curious puppy to investigate them. If you see your dog carrying a piece of vegetation in his mouth, approach him in a quiet, disinterested manner, avoid eye contact, pet him and gradually remove the plant from his mouth. Alternatively, offer him a treat and maybe he'll drop the plant on his own accord. Be sure no toxic plants are growing in your own garden or kept in your home. Ask your vet for information on poisonous plants or research them at your library.

chemicals where the pup cannot reach them.

It is also important to make sure that the outside of your home is safe. Of course, your puppy should never be unsupervised, but a pup let loose in a fenced area will want to run and explore, and he should be granted that freedom. Do not let a fence give you a false sense of security; you would be surprised at how crafty (and persistent) a dog can be in working out how to dig under and squeeze his way through small holes, or to jump or climb over a fence. The breed is not well known for its escapology, but caution should be taken if living in rural areas where livestock may be farmed in view. A sensible fence height of at least 4 feet should be adequate for most Lapphunds. On the other hand, the breed is very talented at digging, and therefore may not suit keen gardeners.

FIRST TRIP TO THE VET
You have selected your puppy, and your home and family are ready. Now all you have to do is collect your Finnish Lapphund from the breeder and the fun begins, right? Well…not so fast. Something else you need to plan is your pup's first trip to the vet. Perhaps the breeder can recommend someone in the area who has experience with the spitz breeds, or maybe you know some other Finnish Lapphund owners who can suggest a good vet. Either way, you should have an appointment arranged for your pup before you pick him up.

The pup's first visit will consist of an overall examination to make sure that the pup does not have any problems that are not apparent to you. The vet will also set up a schedule for the

PUPPY-PROOFING
Thoroughly puppy-proof your house before bringing your puppy home. Never use cockroach or rodent poisons in any area that will be accessible to the dog. Avoid the use of toilet cleaners. Most dogs are born with 'toilet sonar' and will take a drink if the lid is left open. Also keep the rubbish secured and out of reach.

If you don't provide your pup with safe chew toys, you never know what could end up in his mouth. Be a responsible owner and give your puppy proper chew devices.

pup's vaccinations; the breeder will inform you of which ones the pup has already received and the vet can continue from there.

INTRODUCTION TO THE FAMILY
Everyone in the family will be excited about the puppy's coming home and will want to pet him and play with him, but it is best to make the introduction low-key so as not to overwhelm the puppy. He is apprehensive already. It is the first time he has been separated from his mother and the breeder, and the ride to your home is likely to be the first time he has been in a car. The last thing you want to do is smother him, as this will only frighten him further. This is not to say that human contact is not extremely necessary at this stage, because this is the time when a connection between the pup and his human family is formed. Gentle petting and soothing words should help console him, as well as just putting him down and letting him explore on his own (under your watchful eye, of course).

The pup may approach the family members or may busy himself with exploring for a while. Gradually, each person should spend some time with the pup, one at a time, crouching down to get as close to the pup's level as possible, letting him sniff each person's hands and petting him gently. He definitely needs human attention and he needs to be touched—this is how to form an immediate bond. Just remember that the pup is experiencing many things for the first time, at the same time. There are new people, new noises, new smells and new things to investigate, so be gentle, be affectionate and be as comforting as you can be.

PUP'S FIRST NIGHT HOME
You have travelled home with your new charge safely in his crate. He's been to the vet for a thorough check-up; he's been weighed, his papers have been examined and perhaps he's even been vaccinated and wormed as well. He's met (and licked!) the whole family, including the excited children and the less-

A bit of gardening? Pups are natural investigators; keep this in mind when preparing a safe home environment for the new family member.

than-happy cat. He's explored his area, his new bed, the garden and anywhere else he's been permitted. He's eaten his first meal at home and relieved himself in the proper place. He's heard lots of new sounds, smelled new friends and seen more of the outside world than ever before…and that was just the first day! He's worn out and is ready for bed…or so you think!

It's puppy's first night home and you are ready to say 'Good night.' Keep in mind that this is his first night ever to be sleeping alone. His dam and littermates are no longer at paw's length and he's a bit scared, cold and lonely. Be reassuring to your new family member, but this is not the time to spoil him and give in to his inevitable whining.

Puppies whine. They whine to let others know where they are and hopefully to get company out of it. Place your pup in his new bed or crate in his designated area and close the crate door. Mercifully, he may fall asleep without a peep. When the inevitable occurs, however, ignore the whining—he is fine. Be strong and keep his interest in mind. Do not allow yourself to feel guilty and visit the pup. He will fall asleep eventually.

Many breeders recommend placing a piece of bedding from the pup's former home in his new bed so that he recognises and is comforted by the scent of his littermates. Others still advise placing a hot water bottle in the bed for warmth. The latter may be a good idea provided the pup doesn't attempt to suckle—he'll get good and wet, and may not fall asleep so fast.

Puppy's first night can be somewhat stressful for both the pup and his new family.

No task is too big for a puppy with aching gums!

CHEMICAL TOXINS
Scour your garage for potential puppy dangers. Remove weed killers, pesticides and antifreeze materials. Antifreeze is highly toxic and even a few drops can kill a puppy or adult dog. The sweet taste attracts the animal, who will quickly consume it from the floor or kerbside.

FINNISH LAPPHUND

Perhaps the most important life lessons are those taught to the puppies by the dam before the pups leave for new homes.

Remember that you are setting the tone of night-time at your house. Unless you want to play with your pup every night at 10 p.m., midnight and 2 a.m., don't initiate the habit. Your family will thank you, and so will your pup!

PREVENTING PUPPY PROBLEMS

SOCIALISATION
Now that you have done all of the preparatory work and have helped your pup get accustomed to his new home and family, it is about time for you to have some fun! Socialising your Finnish Lapphund pup gives you the opportunity to show off your new friend—surely you are the first owner of a Finnish Lapphund in your neighbourhood—and your pup gets to reap the benefits of being an adorable furry teddy bear that people will want to pet and, in general, think is absolutely precious!

Besides getting to know his new family, your puppy should be exposed to other people, animals and situations. This will help him become well adjusted as he grows up and less prone to being timid or fearful of the new things he will encounter. Of course, he must not come into close contact with dogs you don't know well until his course of injections is fully complete.

Your pup's socialisation began with the breeder, but now it is your responsibility to continue it. The socialisation he receives until the age of 12 weeks is the most critical, as this is the time when he forms his impressions of the outside world. Be especially careful during the eight-to-ten-week-old period, also known as the fear period. The interaction he receives during this time should

> **PUP MEETS WORLD**
> Thorough socialisation includes not only meeting new people but also being introduced to new experiences such as riding in the car, having his coat brushed, hearing the television, walking in a crowd—the list is endless. The more your pup experiences, and the more positive the experiences are, the less of a shock and the less frightening it will be for your pup to encounter new things.

be gentle and reassuring. Lack of socialisation, and/or negative experiences during the socialisation period, can manifest itself in fear and aggression as the dog grows up. Your puppy needs lots of positive interaction, which of course includes human contact, affection, handling and exposure to other animals.

Once your pup has received his necessary vaccinations, feel free to take him out and about (on his lead, of course). Walk him around the neighbourhood, take him on your daily errands, let people pet him, let him meet other dogs and pets, etc. Puppies do not have to try to make friends; there will be no shortage of people who will want to introduce themselves. Just make sure that you carefully supervise each meeting. If the neighbourhood children want to say hello, for example, that is great—children and pups most often make great companions. However, sometimes an excited child can unintentionally handle a pup too roughly, or an overzealous pup can playfully nip a little too hard. You want to make socialisation experiences positive ones. What a pup learns during this very formative stage will affect his attitude toward future encounters. You want your dog to be comfortable around everyone. A pup that has a bad experience with a child may grow up to be a dog that is shy around or aggressive toward children.

CONSISTENCY IN TRAINING

Dogs, being pack animals, naturally need a leader, or else they try to establish dominance in their packs. When you welcome a dog into your family, the choice of who becomes the leader and who becomes the 'pack' is entirely up to you! Your

> **MANNERS MATTER**
>
> During the socialisation process, a puppy should meet people, experience different environments and definitely be exposed to other canines. Through playing and interacting with other dogs, your puppy will learn lessons, ranging from controlling the pressure of his jaws by biting his littermates to the innerworkings of the canine pack that he will apply to his human relationships for the rest of his life. That is why removing a puppy from its litter too early (before eight weeks) can be detrimental to the pup's development.

pup's intuitive quest for dominance, coupled with the fact that it is nearly impossible to look at an adorable Finnish Lapphund pup with his teddy-bear face and not cave in, give the pup almost an unfair advantage in getting the upper hand!

A pup will definitely test the waters to see what he can and cannot do. Do not give in to those pleading eyes—stand your ground when it comes to disciplining the pup and make sure that all family members do the same. It will only confuse the pup if Mother tells him to get off the sofa when he is used to sitting up there with Father to watch the nightly news. Avoid discrepancies by having all members of the household decide on the rules before the pup even comes home…and be consistent in enforcing them! Early training shapes the dog's personality, so you cannot be unclear in what you expect.

Tug-of-war, anyone? Take advantage of your pup's natural curiosity and playfulness to spend quality fun time together…or else he will invent his own games!

COMMON PUPPY PROBLEMS

The best way to prevent puppy problems is to be proactive in stopping an undesirable behaviour as soon as it starts. The old saying 'You can't teach an old dog new tricks' does not necessarily hold true, but it *is* true that it is much easier to discourage bad behaviour in a young developing pup than to wait until the pup's bad behaviour becomes the adult dog's bad habit. There are some problems that are especially prevalent in puppies as they develop.

NIPPING

As puppies start to teethe, they feel the need to sink their teeth into anything available…unfortunately, that usually includes your fingers, arms, hair and toes. You may find this behaviour cute for the first five seconds… until you feel just how sharp those puppy teeth are. Nipping is something you want to discourage immediately and consistently with a firm 'No!' (or whatever number of firm 'Nos' it takes for him to understand that you mean business). Then, replace your finger with an appropriate chew toy. While this behaviour is merely annoying when the dog is young, it can become dangerous as your Finnish Lapphund's adult teeth grow in and his jaws develop, and he continues to think it is

PUPPY PROBLEMS

The majority of problems that are commonly seen in young pups will disappear as your dog gets older. However, how you deal with problems when he is young will determine how he reacts to discipline as an adult dog. It is important to establish who is boss (hopefully it will be you!) right away when you are first bonding with your dog. This bond will set the tone for the rest of your life together.

okay to gnaw on human appendages. Your Finnish Lapphund does not mean any harm with a friendly nip, but he also does not know his own strength.

CRYING/WHINING

Your pup will often cry, whine, whimper, howl or make some type of commotion when he is left alone. This is basically his way of calling out for attention to make sure that you know he is there and that you have not forgotten about him. Your puppy feels insecure when he is left alone, when you are out of the house and he is in his crate or when you are in another part of the house and he cannot see you. The noise he is making is an expression of the anxiety he feels at being alone, so he needs to be taught that being alone is okay. You are not actually training the dog to stop making noise; rather, you are training him to feel comfortable when he is alone and thus removing the need for him to make the noise.

This is where the crate with cosy bedding and a toy comes in handy. You want to know that your pup is safe when you are not there to supervise, and you know that he will be safe in his crate rather than roaming freely about the house. In order for the pup to stay in his crate without making a fuss, he first needs to be comfortable in his crate. On that note, it is extremely important that the crate is never used as a form of punishment; this will cause the pup to view the crate as a negative place rather than as a place of his own for safety and retreat.

Accustom the pup to the crate in short, gradually increasing time intervals in which you put him in the crate, maybe with a treat, and stay in the room with him. If he cries or makes a fuss, do not go to him, but stay in his sight. Gradually he will realise that staying in his crate is okay without your help, and it will not be so traumatic for him when you are not around. You may want to leave the radio on softly when you leave the house; the sound of human voices may be comforting to him.

EVERYDAY CARE OF YOUR FINNISH LAPPHUND

FEEDING YOUR FINNISH LAPPHUND

The actual type of food that you choose to feed your Lapphund will depend on your own personal preferences. Some owners prefer to use natural diets, including fresh meat, vegetables and a carbohydrate such as wholemeal biscuit, bread or pasta; others prefer to use a complete-formula diet as sold in many pet shops. Whichever diet you choose to adopt, it is crucial to remember that the diet must be balanced. That is, it must contain all of the essential ingredients needed for a healthy body and mind, and these ingredients need to be in the correct proportions. So if you choose to feed 'naturally,' it is necessary to ensure that you are aware of all the relevant ingredients—proteins, carbohydrates, fats, roughage, minerals and vitamins—that the dog requires to remain healthy. Also, if you choose to feed a complete formula, you must ensure that the type is suitable for your dog; for example, puppies need different proportions of certain nutrients than a mature adult needs.

The commercial brands are designed with the age of your growing dog in mind. The age at which to shift a puppy from a puppy food to an adult food depends to some extent on the manufacturer's recommendations, many now having a junior life-

FOOD STORAGE

You must store your dried dog food carefully. Open packages of dog food quickly lose their vitamin value, usually within 90 days of being opened. Mould spores and vermin could also contaminate the food.

cycle stage in their range of foods. Since the breed has completed the main stage of growth by about ten months, this would usually be the time to change to the junior food. Further transition to adult food would then take place at around 18 months of age as the dog approaches maturity, but this depends on whether the dog is in good condition and well bodied.

The level of activity of the individual dog will also affect the type of diet that you need to consider for your dog. If you are working the dog in a physically demanding hobby such as agility or herding, then the dog will need a different diet than that of a more sedentary dog. A dog kennelled outside will also have higher caloric demands than a dog living indoors. These are all factors that need to be considered.

The Finnish Lapphund is generally a breed with a healthy appetite; some can be so greedy that care needs to be taken with what and how much they eat. I have known many Finnish Lapphunds who scavenge while out walking, and some who will hunt small animals with a view to supplementing their own diets. If your dog has a sensitive stomach, then such activities may create problems, and you will need to be more careful when your dog is out on a walk.

Generally, the author finds that the breed is a 'good doer' and can maintain good condition on relatively small amounts of food. For instance, an adult bitch needs about 8 ounces of a quality complete adult diet. However, whether it is the dog's wild instincts driving it to eat for survival or just sheer greed, the Lapphund will often appear to still be hungry after its allotted portion. This should not be viewed by the caring owner as an invitation to overfeed his pet. Since a fat dog is not a healthy dog, this aspect of the diet needs to be carefully monitored.

When buying your puppy, the breeder should provide you with a puppy diet sheet and a sufficient quantity of the puppy's current diet to enable you to feed it over the first few days in its new home without making drastic dietary changes. Any changes that you do wish to make should be carried out gradually so as not to

Take the breeder's advice as to what to feed your new puppy, and make any changes gradually. The breeder should give you a diet sheet to follow.

upset the pup's stomach. The diet sheet should give guidelines for the amounts of food required for your puppy, and ideas of when to reduce the number of meals.

Some people prefer to feed once a day and others prefer a two-meal-a-day plan. The other option of free access to food is not one that the author personally recommends since it tends to encourage fussy and slow feeders. The choice of whether to feed one or two meals a day will probably depend on your own experiences and personal circumstances.

WATER
Just as your dog needs proper nutrition from his food, water is an essential 'nutrient' as well. Water keeps the dog's body properly hydrated and promotes normal function of the body's systems. During house-training, it is necessary to keep an eye on how much water your Finnish Lapphund is drinking, but, once he is reliably trained, he should have access to clean fresh water at all times, especially if you feed dried food only. Make certain that the dog's water bowl is clean, and change the water often.

EXERCISE
The adult Finnish Lapphund is a lively and active dog that will be happy to tackle most forms of exercise and will love to go on long family walks. But it must be remembered that for any athlete, fitness and stamina need to be developed and it would be wrong to suddenly expect your pet to join you on a five-mile jog without any training. Most adult Finnish Lapphunds appreciate at least an hour's walk each day, but can undertake much more, dependent on their own level of fitness. Many Finnish Lapphunds accompany their owners out jogging or bicycle riding.

FEEDING TIPS
Dog food must be served at room temperature, neither too hot nor too cold. Fresh water, changed daily and served in a clean bowl, is mandatory, especially when feeding dried food.

Never feed your dog from the table while you are eating, and never feed your dog leftovers from your own meal. They usually contain too much fat and too much seasoning.

Dogs must chew their food. Hard pellets are excellent; soups and slurries are to be avoided.

Don't add leftovers or any extras to commercial dog food. The normal food is usually balanced, and adding something extra destroys the balance.

Except for age-related changes, dogs do not require dietary variations. They can be fed the same diet, day after day, without becoming bored or ill.

Everyday Care

> **EASY DOES IT**
> On average, a fully mature adult Lapphund will require about one hour of exercise a day. This may be given as two separate periods, or as one, but the breed is certainly capable of enduring much longer spells of exercise. Young maturing puppies should, of course, receive shorter periods of walking, or free running, until their bone structure is developed and they are sufficiently muscled to take the extended exercise. Under the age of ten months, jumping is not advised, as the body weight and muscle development are not necessarily balanced until mature size is reached, and the pup may be easily injured or joints damaged.

With young puppies, the amount of exercise and, more importantly, the type of exercise should be carefully monitored. A puppy out running free in the park will soon indicate when it is tired simply by slowing down, and even by taking breathers and lying down. If the same pup was expected to undertake a brisk walk on the lead, pounding the pavement for long periods of time, then damage may be done to its developing bones and ligaments.

While the puppy is still developing, it is not advised to encourage jumping or climbing/descending stairs, since the shock on the joints caused by landing from a height can result in joint damage. In both agility and working trials, dogs are not permitted to compete until 18 months of age to protect young dogs from the stresses of too much jumping too soon.

GROOMING

COAT MAINTENANCE
Although a fairly heavy-coated breed, the Finnish Lapphund in fact requires relatively little grooming to keep it neat. About a half an hour of routine grooming a week should be sufficient for the pet dog. If the dog is required

A nutritionally complete diet and adequate exercise should keep your Finnish Lapphund in healthy physical condition, at a proper weight.

to be turned out in top condition for the conformation show ring, more time will be demanded. The breed requires no formal trimming or stripping, and no specialist grooming skills should be required to keep your pet looking good.

There are three main areas to consider when grooming the dog. First, the longer coat around the neck, ears and leg furnishings will need regular attention to ensure that the longer soft hair does not mat. For these areas, a medium-bristle brush and medium metal comb should be used. The bristle brush can be used to separate the hair and get through to the softer undercoat, teasing out any matting as required. Then finish off using the metal comb to ensure that there are no remaining knots and that all of the hairs are separated.

For the main body hair, it must be remembered that the breed has a two-layer coat, and because the topcoat is harsh and straight, it is unlikely to mat or knot. The area to which you must pay attention is the thick softer undercoat. Again, using a medium-bristle brush, and parting the hair in sections, brush through the undercoat, making sure that you penetrate to the skin. By working in sections from underneath, you will be able to check that no grass seeds have found their way into the coat and you can check for telltale signs of fleas and other bothersome parasites.

If your pet is regularly walked in areas grazed by sheep or deer or in heavily wooded areas, it is necessary to brush to the root so that you can keep an eye out for ticks, which may penetrate the coat and burrow into the dog's skin. If ticks are found, then care must be taken when removing them. It is necessary to remove the whole tick carefully; if the head becomes detached in the dog, then an abscess is likely to result. Also, the tick itself may harbour certain diseases that are transmittable to man, so wearing gloves is advised and the tick should be disposed of promptly. In North America, Lyme disease is a major concern when dealing with ticks.

Once you are confident that the undercoat is mat-free, then the comb should be used through the topcoat just to ensure that there are no knots there either.

For the tail and trousers (knickers, if you will), remember that the coat at the rear of the Finnish Lapphund tends to be much longer than the main body coat, thus needing more attention to prevent knotting. Few dogs are happy to have this more delicate area groomed, so again it is a necessary part of your puppy's training to familiarise him with the process so that he tolerates

Everyday Care

the task at hand. Some dogs prefer to be groomed standing up, others lying down. All that matters is that the dog should stay still so that you are able to separate the layers of the coat and brush/comb right through to the skin.

With the longer coat in this area, it is advisable to start with the bristle brush and tease out any mats or knots, and then finish off with the comb. Pulling on the long hair with a comb when there are knots will only pull on the dog's skin and cause discomfort, which will make him intolerant of your actions.

The Finnish Lapphund is not a trimmed breed, so your main tools will be the brush, comb and nail clippers. However, some owners do like to trim the excess hair from under the feet, between the pads. This conveniently reduces the amount of hair on the Lapphund's foot to soak up water and mud, thus limiting the number of muddy pawprints in the house. The choice of whether to carry this out is therefore a personal one. Other feathering around the hocks, etc., is very much sought after for the show ring and therefore never should be trimmed.

Being a heavy-coated breed, a Finnish Lapphund moults (sheds) a lot, and it definitely gets noticed about the house! To minimise the impact on your

Brushing the tail feathering up toward the tip of the tail will accentuate the trademark plume.

A gentle comb-through following brushing will help rid the coat of mats and tangles.

Be very careful as you comb the furnishings, such as the longer hair on the ears.

FINNISH LAPPHUND

Your local pet shop should have an ample selection of grooming tools from which you can select those you need for maintaining your Finnish Lapphund's coat.

vacuum cleaner, it is advisable to strip out the loose hair as quickly as possible. This can be best achieved by using a pin brush or stripping brush on the soft undercoat once it has started to clump and shed. You will know the time is right when your Lapphund starts to have little tufts/clumps of hair hanging and ultimately dropping onto the carpet. You are well advised to do this job outside.

Part the dog's coat and then gently use the pin brush on the coat, working in the direction of the hair, i.e. brushing away from the roots. You will soon have a very satisfied feeling when you are left with one much thinner-looking Lapphund and a pile of soft hair. Many believe that the quicker the dog is stripped out, the quicker the new coat will grow. Also, if the tufts are left on the dog, they will only mat and make the task of grooming more difficult in the long run.

Another useful tool for grooming such an heavy-coated breed is a blaster, like an hair dryer, which can be used on a dry dog as well as a wet one. The blaster does not produce hot drying air, simply a high-pressure jet of air that either blows away dirt and dead hair, or water in the case of a wet dog. The author has found it an invaluable tool, as the powerful air jet quickly gets to the hair roots and lifts loose dead

PHOTO COURTESY OF MIKKI PET PRODUCTS.

Everyday Care

hair without the constant need to brush. Again, this is a job that is much better done outside.

For the occasional muddy dog, the chore is simpler than you might expect. The coat of the Finnish Lapphund is very weather- and mud-resistant. If your dog becomes wet or muddy, then simply use a towel to remove the worst, and then leave the rest to dry. Once the coat is dry, you will be surprised how easily the mud will fall away or be brushed from the dog.

Regular grooming of your dog is necessary for the care and welfare of his coat and general health, but it also provides a very important bonding time, with you and the dog learning to accept and work with each other. If you are unable to fully groom and care for your dog, then it shows that there is not full trust and understanding between the two of you and other training issues may soon arise. It is therefore wise to start all of these grooming habits very early on with your puppy to build up the bond between you both and minimise confrontations at a later age.

BATHING

Dogs do not need to be bathed as often as humans, but occasional bathing when the need arises is important for clean skin and a healthy coat. Again, like most anything, if you accustom your pup to being bathed as a puppy, it will be second nature by the time he grows up. You want your dog to be at ease in the bath or else it could end up a wet, soapy, messy ordeal for both of you!

Brush your Finnish Lapphund thoroughly before wetting his coat. This will get rid of most mats and tangles, which are harder to remove when the coat is wet. Make certain that your dog has a good non-slip surface on which to stand. Begin by wetting the dog's coat, checking the water temperature to make sure that it is neither too hot nor too cold for the dog. A

Grooming with a hair dryer makes brushing less of a chore, as the air jet removes much debris and dead hair from the coat.

FINNISH LAPPHUND

Your dog's teeth should be checked regularly. Initiate a home dental-care routine in between visits to the vet.

Use a soft cotton wipe to remove tear stains or anything that accumulates in the corners of the eyes.

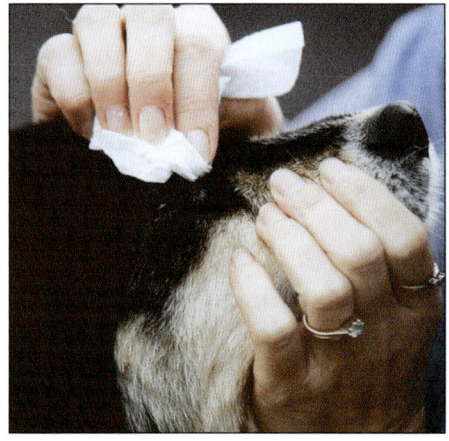

shower or hose attachment is necessary for thoroughly wetting and rinsing the coat.

Next, apply shampoo to the dog's coat and work it into a good lather. Wash the head last, as you do not want shampoo to drip into the dog's eyes while you are washing the rest of his body. You should use only a shampoo that is made for dogs. Do not use a product made for human hair, as these products are too harsh and will strip away the essential oils that make the dog water-resistant. Work the shampoo all the way down to the skin. You can use this opportunity to check the skin for any bumps, bites or other abnormalities. Do not neglect any area of the body—get all of the hard-to-reach places.

Once the dog has been thoroughly shampooed, he requires an equally thorough rinsing. Shampoo left in the coat can be irritating to the dog's skin. Protect his eyes from the shampoo by shielding them with your hand and directing the flow of water in the opposite direction. You also should avoid getting water in the ear canal. Be prepared for your dog to shake out his coat—you might want to stand back, but make sure you have a hold on the dog to keep him from running through the house.

TEETH

Regular checks and cleaning are required to ensure that tartar does not build up and lead to gum infections. While your puppy is young, get him used to your brushing his teeth, either using a specialist canine tooth-

Everyday Care

brush (available from pet shops) or a soft cloth, combined with doggy toothpaste. Gentle rubbing of the teeth will help prevent tartar build-up. Dogs who gnaw on fresh bones or hard toys designed to assist in keeping the dog's teeth clean will require less cleaning, but certainly as a dog gets older and more reluctant to chew on bones or hard foods, cleaning becomes more necessary. Therefore, it is best to train your dog to accept tooth cleaning when he is still young.

Eyes

A moist tissue or wad of cotton can be used to remove any sticky material in the corner of the eyes. With paler coloured dogs, tear stains may become apparent at the corners of the eyes if there is excessive tear production, requiring extra attention. This is usually more common in breeds with prominent eyes or tight-fitting eyelids, something that should not be an issue with the Finnish Lapphund.

Ears

Regular checks should be made to ensure that the insides of the ears are clean, and free of mites and debris. The Finnish Lapphund has small neat ears that are not inclined to attract foreign bodies like grass seeds, but, of course, if you exercise your dog in areas where there is a lot of grass seed (small darts), then particular attention should be made to these checks.

Anal Region

You should regularly check that this area is clean and free of excreta. While the breed is heavily coated in this region, this does not cause any specific problems. Obviously, though, if the dog has a bout of diarrhoea, extra cleaning of the coat in this region with warm water may be required. Be sure that the dog's anal glands are functioning properly and not becoming impacted. If you see your dog dragging his bottom along the floor, then you should have the vet inspect the anal

A wad of cotton, along with ear cleansing liquid or powder for dogs, can be used to clean the outer ear. Never enter the ear canal itself; this can cause injury.

FINNISH LAPPHUND

Have the dog comfortable on the grooming table and hold his foot in your hand as you clip his nails.

Purchase nail clippers made especially for dogs. With the guillotine type, the tip of the nail is inserted into the clipper and taken off in one quick clip.

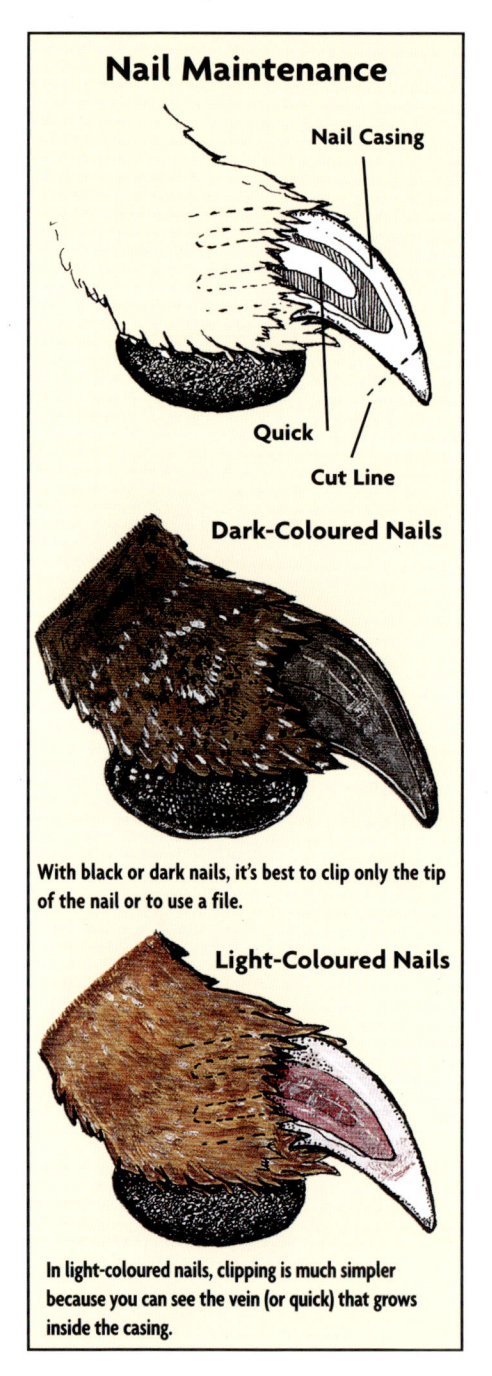

Nail Maintenance

Nail Casing

Quick

Cut Line

Dark-Coloured Nails

With black or dark nails, it's best to clip only the tip of the nail or to use a file.

Light-Coloured Nails

In light-coloured nails, clipping is much simpler because you can see the vein (or quick) that grows inside the casing.

Everyday Care 97

glands. These can be expressed to relieve any accumulated faecal matter.

NAILS

All puppies should be trained from an early age to accept routine nail trimming, but if the dog is regularly exercised on hard surfaces (pavement), then you will find that nail trimming is a very infrequently required grooming chore. The contact of the nails on the hard surface is sufficient to keep the nails naturally trimmed. However, the front dewclaws (and rear, if present) will require regular trimming; once a month should be adequate.

Care should be taken to remove only the tip of the nail, and not to crush or cut into the nail quick, where the blood vessels occur, since this will be painful for the dog and will cause the nail to bleed profusely. As dogs become older and require less exercise, you may find that the nails require more regular trimming, so, again, it is wise to get your dog used to this procedure while still young.

TRAVELLING WITH YOUR DOG

CAR TRAVEL

You should accustom your Finnish Lapphund to riding in a car at an early age. You may or may not take him in the car often, but at the very least he will need to go to the vet and you do not want these trips to be traumatic for the dog or troublesome for you. The safest way for a dog to ride in the car is in his crate. If he uses a crate in the house, you can

Never drive with your Finnish Lapphund unsecured in your car. A crate is the safest option, yet another benefit of crate training your dog.

Here's a clever way to give your dog some fresh air and room to stretch during stops, but only when you're there to supervise.

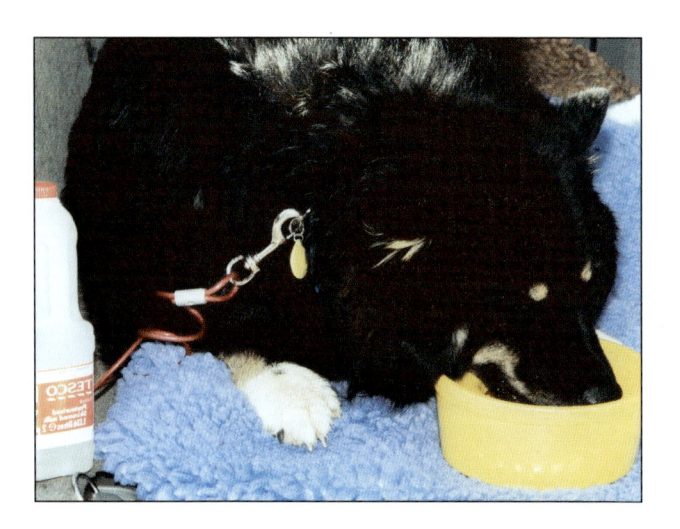

Always have water available to your dog while travelling. Bring cold bottled water along from home and stop frequently to offer him a drink.

use the same crate for travel.

Put the pup in the crate and see how he reacts. If he seems uneasy, you can have a passenger hold him on his lap while you drive. Another option for car travel is a specially made safety harness for dogs, which straps the dog in much like a seat belt. Do not let the dog roam loose in the vehicle—this is very dangerous! If you should stop short, your dog can be thrown and injured. If the dog starts climbing on you and pestering you while you are driving, you will not be able to concentrate on the road. It is an unsafe situation for everyone—human and canine.

For long trips, be prepared to make stops to let the dog relieve himself, and always keep him on-lead when out of the car. Take with you whatever you need to clean up after him, including some paper towels and perhaps some old towelling for use should he have a toileting accident in the car or suffer from motion sickness.

AIR TRAVEL

For all flights, the dog will be required to travel in a fibreglass crate and you should always check in advance with the airline regarding specific requirements. To help put the dog at ease, give him one of his favourite toys in the crate. Do not feed the dog for several hours before the trip in order to minimise his need to relieve himself. However, certain regulations specify that water must always be made available to the dog in the crate.

Make sure that your dog is properly identified and that your contact information as well as any other required labelling appears on his crate. Of course, he should be wearing his ID tags with your contact information as well. Dogs travel in a different area of the plane than human passengers, so every rule must be strictly followed so as to prevent the risk of getting separated from your dog.

BOARDING

So you want to take a long family weekend—and you want to include *all* members of the family. You would probably make arrangements for accommodations ahead of time anyway, but this is especially important when travelling with a dog. You do not want to make an overnight stop at the only place around for miles, only to find out that they do not allow dogs. Also, you do not want to reserve a place for your family without confirming that you are travelling with a dog, because, if it is against their policy, you may end up without a place to stay.

Alternatively, if you are travelling and choose not to take your Finnish Lapphund, you will have to make arrangements for him while you are away. Some options are to take him to a neighbour's house to stay while you are gone, to have a trusted neighbour stop by often or stay at your house or to take your dog to a reputable boarding kennel. Quite possibly, your vet will have a boarding facility at his clinic. If you choose to board him at a kennel, you should visit in advance to see the facilities provided and where the dogs are kept. Are the dogs' areas spacious and kept clean? Talk to some of the employees and observe how they treat the dogs—do they spend time with the dogs, play with them, exercise them, etc.? Also find out the kennel's policy on vaccinations and what they require. This is for all of the dogs' safety, since there is a greater risk of diseases being passed from dog to dog when dogs are kept together.

IDENTIFICATION
Your Finnish Lapphund is your valued companion and friend. That is why you always keep a close eye on him and you have made sure that he cannot escape from his fenced area or wriggle out of his collar and run away from you. However, accidents can happen and there may come a time when your dog unexpectedly becomes separated from you. If this unfortunate event should occur, the first thing on your mind will be finding him. Proper identification, including an ID tag, and possibly a tattoo and/or a microchip, will increase the chances of his being returned to you safely and quickly.

Your dog should never be without his identification tag on his everyday collar, except during bathing and grooming.

TRAINING YOUR
FINNISH LAPPHUND

Your Finnish Lapphund puppy is ready and waiting to soak up whatever you have to teach him, so take this responsibility seriously.

The same is true with your Finnish Lapphund. Any dog is a big responsibility and, if not trained sensibly, may develop unacceptable behaviour that annoys you or could even cause family friction.

To train your Finnish Lapphund, you may like to enrol in an obedience class. Teach your dog good manners as you learn how and why he behaves the way he does. Find out how to communicate with your dog and how to recognise and understand his communications with you. Suddenly the dog takes on a new role in your life—he is clever, interesting, well behaved and fun to be with. He demonstrates his bond of devotion to you daily. In

Living with an untrained dog is a lot like owning a piano that you do not know how to play—it is a nice object to look at, but it does not do much more than that to bring you pleasure. Now try taking piano lessons, and suddenly the piano comes alive and brings forth magical sounds and rhythms that set your heart singing and your body swaying.

TRAINING TIP
Dogs will do anything for your attention. If you reward the dog when he is attentive and calm, you will develop a well-mannered dog. If, on the other hand, you greet your dog excitedly and encourage him to wrestle with you, the dog will greet you the same way and you will have an hyperactive dog on your hands.

other words, your Finnish Lapphund does wonders for your ego because he constantly reminds you that you are not only his leader, you are his hero!

Those involved with teaching dog obedience and counselling owners about their dogs' behaviour have discovered some interesting facts about dog ownership. For example, training dogs when they are puppies results in the highest rate of success in developing well-mannered and well-adjusted adult dogs. Training an older dog, from six months to six years of age, can produce almost equal results, providing that the owner accepts the dog's slower rate of learning capability and is willing to work patiently to help the dog succeed at developing to his fullest potential. Unfortunately, many owners of untrained adult dogs lack the patience factor, so they do not persist until their dogs are successful at learning particular behaviours.

Training a puppy aged 10 to 16 weeks (20 weeks at the most) is like working with a dry sponge in a pool of water. The pup soaks up whatever you show him and constantly looks for more things to do and learn. At this early age, his body is not yet producing hormones, and therein lies the reason for such a high rate of success. Without hormones, he is focused on his owners and not particularly interested in investigating other places, dogs, people, etc. You are his leader: his provider of food, water, shelter and security. He latches onto you and wants to stay close. He will usually follow you from room to room, will not let you out of his sight when you are outdoors with him and will respond in like manner to the people and animals you encounter. If you greet a friend warmly, he will be happy to greet the person as well. If,

REAP THE REWARDS
If you start with a normal, healthy dog and give him time, patience and some carefully executed lessons, you will reap the rewards of that training for the life of the dog. And what a life it will be! The two of you will find immeasurable pleasure in the companionship you have built together with love, respect and understanding.

however, you are hesitant or anxious about the approach of a stranger, he will respond accordingly.

Once the puppy begins to produce hormones, his natural curiosity emerges and he begins to investigate the world around him. It is at this time when you may notice that the untrained dog begins to wander away from you and even ignore your commands to stay close. When this behaviour becomes a problem, you have two choices: get rid of the dog or train him. It is strongly urged that you choose the latter option.

You usually will be able to find obedience classes within a reasonable distance from your home, but you can also do a lot to train your dog yourself. Sometimes there are classes available, but the tuition is too costly. Whatever the circumstances, the solution to training your dog without obedience formal classes lies within the pages of this book.

This chapter is devoted to helping you train your Finnish Lapphund at home. If the recommended procedures are followed faithfully, you may expect positive results that will prove rewarding both to you and your dog.

Whether your new charge is a puppy or a mature adult, the methods of teaching and the techniques we use in training basic behaviours are the same. After all,

> **HIS OWN LITTLE CORNER**
> Mealtime should be a peaceful time for your puppy. Do not put his food and water bowls in an high-traffic area in the house. For example, give him his own little corner of the kitchen where he can eat undisturbed and where he will not be underfoot. Do not allow small children or other family members to disturb the pup when he is eating.

no dog, whether puppy or adult, likes harsh or inhumane methods. All creatures, however, respond favourably to gentle motivational methods and sincere praise and encouragement. Now let us get started.

HOUSE-TRAINING
You can train a puppy to relieve himself wherever you choose, but this must be somewhere suitable. You should bear in mind from the outset that when your puppy is old enough to go out in public places, any canine deposits must be removed at once. You will always have to carry with you a small plastic bag or 'poop-scoop.'

Outdoor training includes such surfaces as grass, soil and cement. Indoor training usually means training your dog to newspaper. When deciding on the surface and location that you will want your Finnish Lapphund to

# Training

use, be sure it is going to be permanent. Training your dog to grass and then changing your mind a few months later is extremely difficult for both dog and owner.

Next, choose the command you will use each and every time you want your puppy to void. 'Hurry up' and 'Let's go' are examples of commands commonly used by dog owners. Get in the habit of giving the puppy your chosen relief command before you take him out. That way, when he becomes an adult, you will be able to determine if he wants to go out when you ask him. A confirmation will be signs of interest, such as wagging his tail, watching you intently, going to the door, etc.

PUPPY'S NEEDS

The puppy needs to relieve himself after play periods, after each meal, after he has been sleeping and at any time he indicates that he is looking for a place to urinate or defecate. The urinary and intestinal tract muscles of very young puppies are not fully developed. Therefore, like human babies, puppies need to relieve themselves frequently.

Take your puppy out often—every hour for an eight-week-old, for example—and always immediately after sleeping and eating. The older the puppy, the less often he will need to relieve

HONOUR AND OBEY

Dogs are the most honourable animals in existence. They consider another species (humans) as their own. They interface with you. You are their leader. Puppies perceive children to be on their level; their actions around small children are different from their behaviour around their adult masters.

Puppies learn the house-training routine quickly... don't miss the signs! If your pup is waiting by the door, there's a reason.

himself. Finally, as a mature healthy adult, he will require only three to five relief trips per day.

HOUSING
Since the types of housing and control you provide for your puppy have a direct relationship on the success of house-training, we consider the various aspects of both before we begin training.

Taking a new puppy home and turning him loose in your house can be compared to turning a child loose in an exhibition centre and telling the child that the place is all his! The sheer enormity of the place would be too much for him to handle.

Instead, offer the puppy clearly defined areas where he can play, sleep, eat and live. A room of the house where the family gathers is the most obvious choice. Puppies are social animals and need to feel a part of the pack right from the start. Hearing your voice, watching you while you are doing things and smelling you nearby are all positive reinforcers that he is now a member of your pack. Usually a family room, the kitchen or a nearby adjoining breakfast area is ideal for providing safety and security for both puppy and owner.

Within the designated room, there should be a smaller area that the puppy can call his own. An alcove, a wire or fibreglass dog crate or a partitioned (not boarded!) corner from which he can view the activities of his new family will be fine. The size of the area or crate is the key factor here. The area must be large enough so that the puppy can lie down and stretch out, as well as stand up, without rubbing his head on the top. At the same time, it must be small enough so that he cannot relieve himself at one end and sleep at the other without coming into contact with his droppings before he is fully trained to relieve himself outside. Dogs are, by nature, clean animals and will not remain close to their relief areas unless forced to do so. In those cases, they then become

CANINE DEVELOPMENT TIMETABLE

It is important to understand how and at what age a puppy develops into adulthood. If you are a puppy owner, consult the following Canine Development Timetable to determine the stage of development your puppy is currently experiencing. This knowledge will help you as you work with the puppy in the weeks and months ahead.

Period	Age	Characteristics
First to Third	Birth to Seven Weeks	Puppy needs food, sleep and warmth, and responds to simple and gentle touching. Needs mother for security and disciplining. Needs littermates for learning and interacting with other dogs. Pup learns to function within a pack and learns pack order of dominance. Begin socialising pup with adults and children for short periods. Pup begins to become aware of its environment.
Fourth	Eight to Twelve Weeks	Brain is fully developed. Needs socialising with outside world. Remove from mother and littermates. Needs to change from canine pack to human pack. Human dominance necessary. Fear period occurs between 8 and 12 weeks. Avoid fright and pain.
Fifth	Thirteen to Sixteen Weeks	Training and formal obedience should begin. Less association with other dogs, more with people, places, situations. Period will pass easily if you remember this is pup's change-to-adolescence time. Be firm and fair. Flight instinct prominent. Permissiveness and over-disciplining can do permanent damage. Praise for good behaviour.
Juvenile	Four to Eight Months	Another fear period about 7 to 8 months of age. It passes quickly, but be cautious of fright and pain. Sexual maturity reached. Dominant traits established. Dog should understand sit, down, come and stay by now.

NOTE: THESE ARE APPROXIMATE TIME FRAMES. ALLOW FOR INDIVIDUAL DIFFERENCES IN PUPPIES.

dirty dogs and usually remain that way for life.

The dog's designated area should contain clean bedding and a toy. Once house-training is accomplished, water must always be available in his area, in a non-spill container. Before the pup is house-trained, only offer food and water outside his area.

CONTROL
By *control*, we mean helping the puppy to create a lifestyle pattern that will be compatible to that of his human pack *(you!)*. Just as we guide little children to learn our way of life, we must show the puppy when it is time to play, eat, sleep, exercise and even entertain himself.

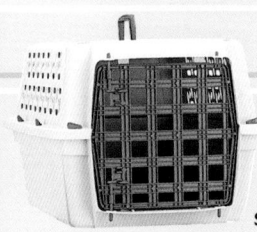

THE SUCCESS METHOD

Success that comes by luck is usually short-lived. Success that comes by well-thought-out proven methods is often more easily achieved and permanent. This is the Success Method. It is designed to give you, the puppy owner, a simple yet proven way to help your puppy develop clean living habits and a feeling of security in his new environment.

6 Steps to Successful Crate Training

1 Tell the puppy 'Crate time!' and place him in the crate with a small treat (a piece of cheese or half of a biscuit). Let him stay in the crate for five minutes while you are in the same room. Then release him and praise lavishly. Never release him when he is fussing. Wait until he is quiet before you let him out.

2 Repeat Step 1 several times a day.

3 The next day, place the puppy in the crate as before. Let him stay there for ten minutes. Do this several times.

4 Continue building time in five-minute increments until the puppy stays in his crate for 30 minutes with you in the room. Always take him to his relief area after prolonged periods in his crate.

5 Now go back to Step 1 and let the puppy stay in his crate for five minutes, this time while you are out of the room.

6 Once again, build crate time in five-minute increments with you out of the room. When the puppy will stay willingly in his crate (he may even fall asleep!) for 30 minutes with you out of the room, he will be ready to stay in it for several hours at a time.

Training

A pup left to his own devices will find plenty of mischief, which is why the crate is always helpful in keeping your young Lapphund safe and out of trouble when you're not able to supervise.

Your puppy should always sleep in his crate. He should also learn that, during times of household confusion and excessive human activity, such as at breakfast when family members are preparing for the day, he can play by himself in relative safety and comfort in his designated area. Each time you leave the puppy alone, he should understand exactly where he is to stay.

Puppies are chewers and cannot tell the difference between lamp and television leads, shoes, table legs, etc. Chewing into a television lead, for example, can be fatal to the puppy, while a shorted lead can start a fire in the house. If the puppy chews on the arm of the chair when he is alone, you will probably discipline him angrily when you get home. Thus, he makes the association that your coming home means he is going to be punished. (He will not remember chewing the chair and is incapable of making the association of the discipline with his naughty deed.) Accustoming the pup to his designated area not only keeps him safe but also avoids his engaging in destructive behaviours when you are not around.

Times of excitement, such as special occasions, family parties, etc., can be fun for the puppy, providing that he can view the activities from the security of his designated area. He is not underfoot and he is not being fed all sorts of titbits that will probably cause him stomach distress, yet he still feels a part of the fun.

ESTABLISHING A RELIEF SCHEDULE
A puppy should be taken to his relief area each time he is released from his designated area, after meals, after play sessions and when he first awakens in the morning (at age eight weeks, this can mean 5 a.m.!). The puppy will indicate that he's ready 'to go' by circling or sniffing busily—do not misinterpret these signs. For a puppy less than ten weeks of age, a routine of taking him out every hour is necessary. As the puppy grows, he will be able to wait for longer periods of time.

Keep trips to his relief area short. Stay no more than five or six minutes and then return to the house. If he goes during that time, praise him lavishly and take him indoors immediately. If he does not, but he has an accident when you go back indoors, pick him up immediately, say 'No! No!' and return to his relief area. Wait a few minutes, then return to the house again. Never hit a puppy or put his face in urine or excrement when he has had an accident!

Once indoors, put the puppy in his crate until you have had time to clean up his accident. Then, release him to the family area and watch him more closely than before. Chances are, his accident was a result of your not picking up his signal or waiting too long before offering him the opportunity to relieve himself. Never hold a grudge against the puppy for accidents.

Let the puppy learn that going outdoors means it is time to relieve himself, not to play. Once trained, he will be able to play indoors and out and still differentiate between the times for play versus the times for relief. Help him develop regular hours for naps, being alone, playing by himself and just resting, all in his crate. Encourage him to entertain himself while you are busy with your activities. Let him learn that

TAKE THE LEAD
Do not carry your dog to his toilet area. Take him there on his lead or, better yet, encourage him to follow you to the spot. If you start carrying him to his spot, you might end up doing this routine forever and your dog will have the satisfaction of having trained *you*.

having you near is comforting, but it is not your main purpose in life to provide him with undivided attention. Each time you put your puppy in his own area, use the same command, whatever suits best. Soon he will run to his crate or special area when he hears you say those words.

Crate training provides safety for you, the puppy and the home. It also provides the puppy with a feeling of security, and that helps the puppy achieve self-confidence and clean habits. Remember that one of the primary ingredients in house-training your puppy is control. Regardless of your lifestyle, there will always be occasions when you will need to have a place where your dog can stay and be happy and safe. Crate training is the answer for now and in the future.

In conclusion, a few key elements are really all you need for a successful house-training method—consistency, frequency, praise, control and supervision. By following these procedures with a normal, healthy puppy, you and the puppy will soon be past the stage of accidents and ready to move on to a full and rewarding life together.

ROLES OF DISCIPLINE, REWARD AND PUNISHMENT

Discipline, training one to act in accordance with rules, brings order to life. It is as simple as that. Without discipline, particularly in a group society, chaos will reign supreme and the group will eventually perish. Humans and canines are social animals and need some form of discipline in order to function effectively. They must procure food, reproduce to keep their species going and protect their home base and their young. If there were no discipline in the lives of social animals, they would eventually die from starva-

HOW MANY TIMES A DAY?

AGE	RELIEF TRIPS
To 14 weeks	10
14–22 weeks	8
22–32 weeks	6
Adulthood (dog stops growing)	4

These are estimates, of course, but they are a guide to the *minimum* number of opportunities a dog should have each day to relieve himself.

tion and/or predation by other stronger animals.

In the case of domestic canines, discipline in their lives is needed in order for them to understand how their pack (you and other family members) functions and how they must act in order to survive.

A large humane society in a highly populated area recently surveyed dog owners regarding their satisfaction with their relationships with their dogs. People who had trained their dogs were 75% more satisfied with their pets than those who had never trained their dogs.

Dr Edward Thorndike, a noted psychologist, established *Thorndike's Theory of Learning*, which states that a behaviour that results in a pleasant event tends to be repeated. Furthermore, it concludes that a behaviour that results in an unpleasant event tends not to be repeated. It is this theory upon which training methods are based today. For example, if you manipulate a dog to perform a specific behaviour and reward him for doing it, he is likely to do it again because he enjoyed the end result.

Occasionally, punishment, a penalty inflicted for an offence, is necessary. The best type of punishment often comes from an outside source. For example, a child is told not to touch the oven because he may get burned. He disobeys and touches the oven. In doing so, he receives a burn. From that time on, he respects the heat of the oven and avoids contact with it. Therefore, a behaviour that results in an unpleasant event tends not to be repeated.

A good example of a dog's learning the hard way is the dog who chases the house cat. He is told many times to leave the cat alone, yet he persists in teasing the cat. Then, one day, the dog begins chasing the cat but the cat turns and swipes a claw across the dog's face, leaving the dog

> **SAFETY FIRST**
> While it may seem that the most important things to your dog are eating, sleeping and chewing the upholstery on your furniture, his first concern is actually safety. The domesticated dogs we keep as companions have the same pack instinct as their ancestors who ran free thousands of years ago. Because of this pack instinct, your dog wants to know that he and his pack are not in danger of being harmed, and that his pack has a strong, capable leader. You must establish yourself as the leader early on in your relationship. That way your dog will trust that you will take care of him and the pack, and he will accept your commands without question.

Training

with a painful gash on his nose. The final result is that the dog stops chasing the cat.

TRAINING EQUIPMENT

COLLAR AND LEAD
For a Finnish Lapphund, the collar and lead that you use for training must be one with which you are easily able to work, not too heavy for the dog and perfectly safe.

TREATS
Have a bag of treats on hand; something nutritious and easy to swallow works best. Use a soft treat, a chunk of cheese or a piece of cooked chicken rather than a dry biscuit. By the time the dog has finished chewing a dry treat, he will forget why he is being rewarded in the first place!

Using food rewards will not teach a dog to beg at the table—the only way to teach a dog to beg at the table is to give him food from the table. In training, rewarding the dog with a food treat will help him associate praise and the treats with learning new behaviours that obviously please his owner.

TRAINING BEGINS: ASK THE DOG A QUESTION
In order to teach your dog anything, you must first get his attention. After all, he cannot learn anything if he is looking away from you with his mind on something else.

To get your dog's attention, ask him 'School?' and immediately walk over to him and give him a treat as you tell him 'Good dog.' Wait a minute or two and repeat the routine, this time with a treat in your hand as you approach within a foot of the dog. Do not go directly to him, but stop about a foot short of him and hold out the treat as you ask 'School?' He will see you approaching with a treat in your hand and most

Attention is the key to all endeavours with your dog. A show dog is a good example, as his attention must stay focused on the handler despite the many distractions: people, other dogs, noise, etc.

likely begin walking toward you. As you meet, give him the treat and praise again.

The third time, ask the question, have a treat in your hand and walk only a short distance toward the dog so that he must walk almost all the way to you. As he reaches you, give him the treat and praise again.

By this time, the dog will probably be getting the idea that if he pays attention to you, espe-

> **THINK BEFORE YOU BARK**
> Dogs are sensitive to their masters' moods and emotions. Use your voice wisely when communicating with your dog. Never raise your voice at your dog unless you are trying to correct him. 'Barking' at your dog can become as meaningless as 'dogspeak' is to you.

cially when you ask that question, it will pay off in treats and enjoyable activities for him. In other words, he learns that 'school' means doing great things with you that are fun and that result in positive attention for him.

Remember that the dog does not understand your verbal language; he only recognises sounds. Your question translates to a series of sounds for him, and those sounds become the signal to go to you and pay attention. The dog learns that if he does this, he will get to interact with you plus receive treats and praise.

THE BASIC COMMANDS

TEACHING SIT
Now that you have the dog's attention, attach his lead and hold it in your left hand, and hold a food treat in your right hand. Place your food hand at the dog's nose and let him lick the treat but not take it from you. Say 'Sit' and slowly raise your food hand from

A little 'push' to show the dog the correct sit position...

...and a reward for a job well done!

in front of the dog's nose up over his head so that he is looking at the ceiling. As he bends his head upward, he will have to bend his knees to maintain his balance. As he bends his knees, he will assume a sit position. At that point, release the food treat and praise lavishly with comments such as 'Good dog! Good sit!,' etc. Remember to always praise enthusiastically, because dogs relish verbal praise from their owners and feel so proud of themselves whenever they accomplish a behaviour.

You will not use food forever in getting the dog to obey your commands. Food is only used to teach new behaviours and, once the dog knows what you want when you give a specific command, you will wean him off the food treats but still maintain the verbal praise. After all, you will always have your voice with you, and there will be many times when you have no food rewards but expect the dog to obey.

TEACHING DOWN
Teaching the down exercise is easy when you understand how the dog perceives the down position, and it is very difficult when you do not. Dogs perceive the down position as a submissive one; therefore, teaching the down exercise by using a forceful method can sometimes make the dog develop such a fear of the

DOUBLE JEOPARDY
A dog in jeopardy never lies down. He stays alert on his feet because instinct tells him that he may have to run away or fight for his survival. Therefore, if a dog feels threatened or anxious, he will not lie down. Consequently, it is important to keep the dog calm and relaxed as he learns the down exercise.

down that he either runs away when you say 'Down' or he attempts to snap at the person who tries to force him down.

Have the dog sit close alongside your left leg, facing in the same direction as you are. Hold the lead in your left hand and a food treat in your right. Now place your left hand lightly on the top of the dog's shoulders where they meet above the spinal cord. Do not push down on the dog's shoulders; simply rest your left hand there so you can guide the dog to lie down close to your left leg rather than to swing away from your side when he drops.

Now place the food hand at the dog's nose, say 'Down' very softly (almost a whisper), and slowly lower the food hand to the dog's front feet. When the food hand reaches the floor, begin moving it forward along the floor in front of the dog. Keep talking softly to the dog, saying things like, 'Do you want this treat? You can do this, good dog.' Your reassuring tone of voice will help calm the dog as he tries to follow the food hand in order to get the treat.

When the dog's elbows touch the floor, release the food and praise softly. Try to get the dog to maintain that down position for several seconds before you let him sit up again. The goal here is to get the dog to settle down and not feel threatened in the down position.

TEACHING STAY

It is easy to teach the dog to stay in either a sit or a down position. Again, we use food and praise during the teaching process as we help the dog to understand exactly what it is that we are expecting him to do.

To teach the sit/stay, start with the dog sitting on your left side as before and hold the lead in your left hand. Have a food treat in your right hand and place your food hand at the dog's nose. Say 'Stay' and step out on your right foot to stand directly in front of the dog, toe to toe, as he licks and nibbles the treat. Be sure to keep his head facing upward to maintain the sit position. Count to five and then swing around to stand next to the dog again with him on your left. As soon as you get back to the original position, release the food and praise lavishly.

To teach the down/stay, do the down as previously described. As soon as the dog lies down, say 'Stay' and step out on your right foot just as you did in the sit/stay. Count to five and then return to stand beside the dog with him on your left side. Release the treat

> **CONSISTENCY PAYS OFF**
> Dogs need consistency in their feeding times, exercise and toilet breaks, and in the verbal commands you use. If you use 'Stay' on Monday and 'Stay here, please' on Tuesday, you will confuse your dog. Don't demand perfect behaviour during training classes and then let him have the run of the house the rest of the day. Above all, lavish praise on your pet consistently every time he does something right. The more he feels he is pleasing you, the more willing he will be to learn.

and praise as always.

Within a week or ten days, you can begin to add a bit of distance between you and your dog when you leave him. When you do, use your left hand open with the palm facing the dog as a stay signal, much the same as the hand signal used to stop traffic. Hold the food treat in your right hand as before, but this time the food will not be touching the dog's nose. He will watch the food hand and quickly learn that he is going to get that treat as soon as you return to his side.

When you can stand a few feet away from your dog for 30 seconds, you can then begin building time and distance in both stays. Eventually, the dog can be expected to remain in the stay position for prolonged periods of time until you return to him or call him to you. Always praise lavishly when he stays.

TEACHING COME

As you may realise, the Lapphund can have a streak of independence about it, and this, combined with a strong herding/hunting instinct, can at times make it reluctant to hear the 'come' command. With this in mind, it is important to teach the exercise at an early age when the pup is still very reliant on its owners. You can perhaps make use of the pup's keenness for food to reward the positive recall. If you make teaching 'come' an exciting experience, you should never have a 'student' that does not love the game or that fails to come when called. The secret, it seems, is never to teach the word 'come.'

At times when an owner most wants his dog to come when called, the owner is likely to be upset or anxious and he allows these feelings to come through in the tone of his voice when he calls his dog. Hearing that desperation in his owner's voice, the dog fears the results of going to him and therefore either disobeys outright or runs in the opposite direction. The secret, therefore, is to teach the dog a game and, when you want him to come to you, simply play the game. It is practically a no-fail solution!

'Where are you?' In the unsettling event that your Lapphund has wandered too far, you want to be confident that he will respond to your call.

To begin, have several members of your family take a few food treats and each go into a different room in the house. Everyone takes turns calling the dog, and each person should celebrate the dog's finding him with a treat and lots of happy praise. When a person calls the dog, he is actually inviting the dog to find him and to get a treat as a reward for 'winning.'

'COME'... BACK
Never call your dog to come to you for a correction or scold him when he reaches you. That is the quickest way to turn a come command into 'Go away fast!' Dogs think only in the present tense, and your dog will connect the scolding with coming to you, not with the misbehaviour of a few moments earlier.

A few turns of the 'Where are you?' game and the dog will understand that everyone is playing the game and that each person has a big celebration awaiting the dog's success at locating him or her. Once the dog learns to love the game, simply calling out 'Where are you?' will bring him running from wherever he is when he hears that all-important question.

The come command is recognised as one of the most important things to teach a dog, but there are trainers who work with thousands of dogs and never use the actual word 'come.' Yet these dogs will race to respond to a person who uses the dog's name followed by 'Where are you?' For example, a woman has a 12-year-old companion dog who went blind, but who never fails to locate her owner when asked, 'Where are you?'

Children, in particular, love to play this game with their dogs. Children can hide in smaller places like a shower or bath, behind a bed or under a table. The dog needs to work a little bit harder to find these hiding places, but, when he does, he loves to celebrate with a treat and a tussle with a favourite youngster.

TEACHING HEEL
Heeling means that the dog walks beside the owner without pulling. It takes time and

patience on the owner's part to succeed at teaching the dog that he (the owner) will not proceed unless the dog is walking calmly beside him. Neither pulling out ahead on the lead nor lagging behind is acceptable.

Begin by holding the lead in your left hand as the dog sits beside your left leg. Move the loop end of the lead to your right hand, but keep your left hand short on the lead so that it keeps the dog in close next to you.

Say 'Heel' and step forward on your left foot. Keep the dog close to you and take three steps. Stop and have the dog sit next to you in what we now call the heel position. Praise verbally, but do not touch the dog. Hesitate a moment and begin again with 'Heel,' taking three steps and stopping, at which point the dog is told to sit again.

Your goal here is to have the dog walk those three steps without pulling on the lead. Once he will walk calmly beside you for three steps without pulling, increase the number of steps you take to five. When he will walk politely beside you while you take five steps, you can increase the length of your walk to ten steps. Keep increasing the length of your stroll until the dog will walk quietly beside you without pulling as long as you want him to heel. When you stop heeling, indicate to the dog that the exer-

COMMAND STANCE
Stand up straight and authoritatively when giving your dog commands. Do not issue commands when lying on the floor or lying on your back on the sofa. If you are on your hands and knees when you give a command, your dog will think you are positioning yourself to play.

cise is over by verbally praising as you pet him and say 'OK, good dog.' The 'OK' is used as a release word, meaning that the exercise is finished and the dog is free to relax.

If you are dealing with a dog

HEELING WELL
Teach your dog to heel in an enclosed area. Once you think the dog will obey reliably and you want to attempt advanced obedience exercises such as off-lead heeling, test him in a fenced-in area so he cannot run away.

who insists on pulling you around, simply 'put on your brakes' and stand your ground until the dog realises that the two of you are not going anywhere until he is beside you and moving at your pace, not his. It may take some time just standing there to convince the dog that you are the leader and that you will be the one to decide on the direction and speed of your travel.

Each time the dog looks up at you or slows down to give a slack lead between the two of you, quietly praise him and say, 'Good heel. Good dog.' Eventually, the dog will begin to respond and within a few days he will be walking politely beside you without pulling on the lead. At first, the training sessions should be kept short and very positive; soon the dog will be able to walk nicely with you for increasingly longer distances. Remember also to give the dog free time and the opportunity to run and play when you have finished heel practice.

WEANING OFF FOOD IN TRAINING
Food is used in training new behaviours. Once the dog understands what behaviour goes with a specific command, it is time to start weaning him off the food treats. At first, give a treat after each exercise. Then, start to give a treat only after every other exercise. Mix up the times when you offer a food reward and the times when you only offer praise so that the dog will never know when he is going to receive both food and praise and when he is going to receive only praise. This is called a variable ratio reward system. It proves successful because there is always the chance that the owner will produce a treat, so the dog never stops trying for that reward. No matter what, *always* give verbal praise.

Training

FEAR AGGRESSION

Pups who are subjected to physical abuse during training commonly end up with behavioural problems as adults. One common result of abuse is fear aggression, in which a dog will lash out, bare his teeth, snarl and finally bite someone by whom he feels threatened. For example, your daughter may be playing with the dog one afternoon. As they play hide-and-seek, she backs the dog into a corner and, as she attempts to tease him playfully, he bites her hand. Examine the cause of this behaviour. Did your daughter ever hit the dog? Did someone who resembles your daughter hit or scream at the dog?

Fortunately, fear aggression is relatively easy to correct. Have your daughter engage in only positive activities with the dog, such as feeding, petting and walking. She should not give any corrections or negative feedback. If the dog still growls or cowers away from her, allow someone else to accompany them. After approximately one week, the dog should feel that he can rely on her for many positive things, and he will also be prevented from reacting fearfully towards anyone who might resemble her.

OBEDIENCE CLASSES

It is a good idea to enrol in an obedience class if one is available in your area. If your dog is destined for the show ring, prepartory showing classes would be more appropriate. Many areas have dog clubs that offer basic obedience training as well as preparatory classes for obedience competition. There are also local dog trainers who offer similar classes.

At obedience events, dogs can earn titles at various levels of competition. The beginning levels of obedience competition include basic behaviours such as sit, down, heel, etc. The more advanced levels of competition include jumping, retrieving, scent discrimination and signal work.

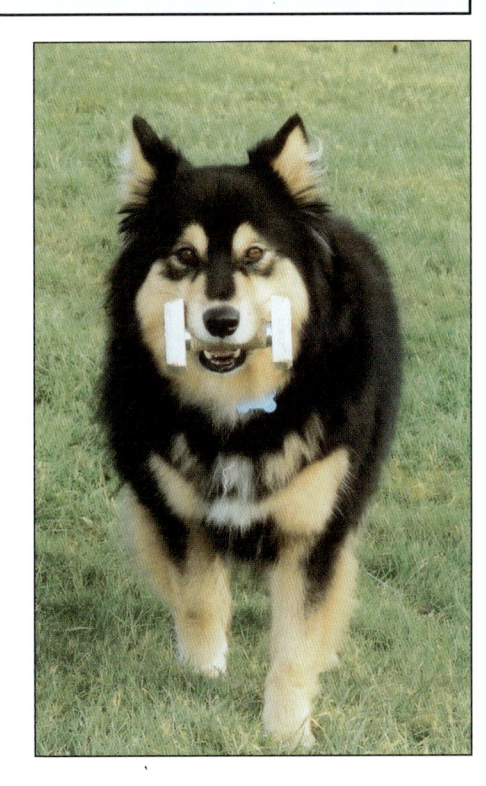

Leemax Herra demonstrates the retrieve with a dumbbell, an advanced obedience exercise.

FINNISH LAPPHUND

The friendly and kind Finnish Lapphund makes a wonderful breed for therapy work. Who wouldn't be comforted by a visit from this delightful dog?

The advanced levels require a dog and owner to put a lot of time and effort into their training. The titles that can be earned at these levels of competition are very prestigious.

TRAINING FOR ACTIVITIES

The breed is extremely versatile and easily trained; therefore, it is suited to all aspects of canine activity, from obedience to agility, from support dog to search and rescue dog, from assistance dog to visiting therapy dog.

THERAPY WORK

The author has had very nice success with her Lapphunds as PAT dogs. Pets as Therapy (PAT) is a National Charity in the UK, which encourages pets to be taken into hospitals, hospices, etc., as therapeutic aids to patients and children, especially where, as a result of long-term hospitalisation, the person has been deprived of the company of his own pets. There are similar organizations in the US such as The Delta Society and the People-Pet Partnership. It is well documented how, in many cases, the action of stroking a pet and regular comforting from a gentle friendly animal can help in the convalescence, healing and therapy of many patients. So it is rewarding to know that Lapphunds have proven themselves suitable for this work.

OBEDIENCE TRIALS

Back home in Finland, Lapphunds have been successful in obedience trials for many years, with perhaps the most noted success being attributed to Mr Rauno Nisula and his two bitches, Finnish & Danish Obedience Ch Hiidenparran Tielkka and Finnish Show Ch and Nordic Obedience Ch Kettuharjun Elle (Nordic title achieved by winning titles from Finland, Norway and Denmark). Elle demonstrates excellent breed type to be a dual champion both for brains and beauty.

Rauno's success in training the breed has meant that he and his bitches have won many awards over more than ten years, with Tielkka winning the Finnish obedience championship finals in 1989 and 1990, and Elle winning in 1998 (she previously picked up the bronze medal in 1995). These major awards represent only a few of their successes, and they have represented Finland in several international finals, competing on the Finnish National Obedience Team around Europe. All together, Elle and Rauno have been in 75 competitions.

Elle was bred by Rauno and there is perhaps little he does not understand about the trainability and characteristics of this breed, having been fortunate to develop two dogs to such high levels. Rauno says that Elle is quite a character and can be very demanding and stubborn, but she is also very clever and is a quick learner. He emphasises that the most important thing in training is to be good friends with your dog, so that when you say that something needs to be or will be done, the dog then understands and follows through with the command—trust and loyalty must work both ways.

Rauno says that he has taught some unusual tricks to Elle, things that many other competitors and friends have laughed about—until the results demonstrated what clever tricks they are!

For example, in the higher obedience competition classes, it has been noted that the 'recall' has resulted in slow recalls, simply because the exercise requires the dogs to sit halfway on their return to their owners. The clever dogs soon learn to anticipate the 'sit' command and return quite slowly, trotting, not galloping happily.

So Rauno taught the command 'Gallop' to Elle, by incorporating the training into their daily walks. Each time Elle was enthusiastically running to

> **PAT CONTACT**
> For information on how your dog can become a PAT dog, contact:
> Pets as Therapy
> 17 Ambrook Road
> Reading RG2 8SL
> England
> Telephone: 0118 9212 467

FINNISH LAPPHUND

Rauno out on their walks, he gave her the command 'Gallop.' Soon Elle learned the command and he began to use it in the competitions. Although it may sound like a funny trick, it worked well for the team. Elle was able to recall happily and at a fast gallop, then stop and do the obligatory sit midway and then complete the recall by galloping all the way to Rauno.

Rauno believes that the Finnish Lapphund is a breed suited to obedience because of its natural herding-dog intelligence, their willingness to please and work with people, their handy size, their natural, healthy and well-constructed bodies and their easy-to-maintain coats.

Success is not restricted to Rauno. On average in Finland, a Finnish Lapphund achieves obedience championship status once a year, and there are now about a dozen obedience title-holders. In addition, there are many competitors enjoying obedience competition at the lower levels.

SEARCH AND RESCUE

Another very noticeable strength of the breed is the ability to track using scent and, for this reason, the breed is used in Finland for

Finnish Show and Nordic Obedience Ch Kettuharjun Elle is one of owner Rauno Nisula's highly successful Finnish Lapphunds.

Swedish, Nordic & Danish Ch Rävrackans Hunaja Hilkka demonstrates 'blood tracking.'

search and rescue of lost walkers and the like, plus tracking injured reindeer.

'Blood tracking' is taught in Sweden for the dogs to track roe deer and elks that have been hurt in road-traffic accidents or to find animals injured in hunting that have not received a clean kill. For training purposes, a track is laid using cow's blood and part of a leg from a slaughtered deer. The leg is dragged behind the track-layer to effectively lay the track (all done without the dog's seeing the track set, of course). Then the track is left for 2 to 24 hours, depending on the experience of the dog, allowing the human smell to disappear and thus training the dog to work to the old blood smells. The dog is then asked to find the track, which can be up to 600 metres in length. At the end of the track, the dog is allowed to find a reward.

During training, gunshots are fired as close as 5 to 10 metres to the dog to ensure that the dog is not gun-shy. These trained dogs then can be used to search for injured animals and enable these animals to be treated for their injuries as necessary, thus reducing their suffering.

AGILITY TRIALS

Agility is yet another canine sport for which the Lapphund is suited, with members of the breed competing at all levels. The dogs are very agile for their size. I liken the Lapphund to the harrier jump jet—capable of a vertical take-off from a standing start—and they certainly are quick to learn the relevance of the contact obstacles. The breed may not be built for the same level of speed over the course as the swift Border Collie, but certainly the Lapphund's lightness of foot and catlike nimbleness along narrow walkways and see-saws mean that he is capable of holding his own in competition.

124   FINNISH LAPPHUND

This Lapphund navigates the agility weave poles with ease.

WORKING TRIALS
Working trials combine many aspects from obedience, tracking and agility, comprising exercises divided into three sections: Control, Agility and Nosework. The control aspects include exercises seen in obedience tests, plus the addition of an exercise testing steadiness to gunshot. The agility obstacles are very demanding of the dog's physical strength and include a 6-foot scale and a 9-foot-long jump. For tracking, a track over approximately half a mile is laid, and the dog is expected to follow the set pattern and recover articles that have been placed along the track. There is also a nosework exercise consisting of a marked area in which the dog must systematically search the

Finnish Lapphunds stay active into old age, as this high-flying veteran demonstrates as he clears the tyre jump.

Skiiers can include their Lapphunds, as this versatile breed is well suited to the snow and can be trained for most anything.

area and recover various articles. For more senior dogs, the qualification can require 'manwork,' with the dog's being required to find a hidden person, restrain a person and the like.

Choose Your Activity

The Finnish Lapphund is a breed that thoroughly enjoys the challenge of learning and the rewards of pleasing its owners, so taking up a canine hobby with your dog will benefit both you and your dog. Each activity has a different training requirement—some require you to start with very young dogs, while others are better suited to older dogs. If you are interested in developing your dog's talents and giving him a full and varied life, then contact your national kennel club or breed club for more information on the various types of events and how to become involved.

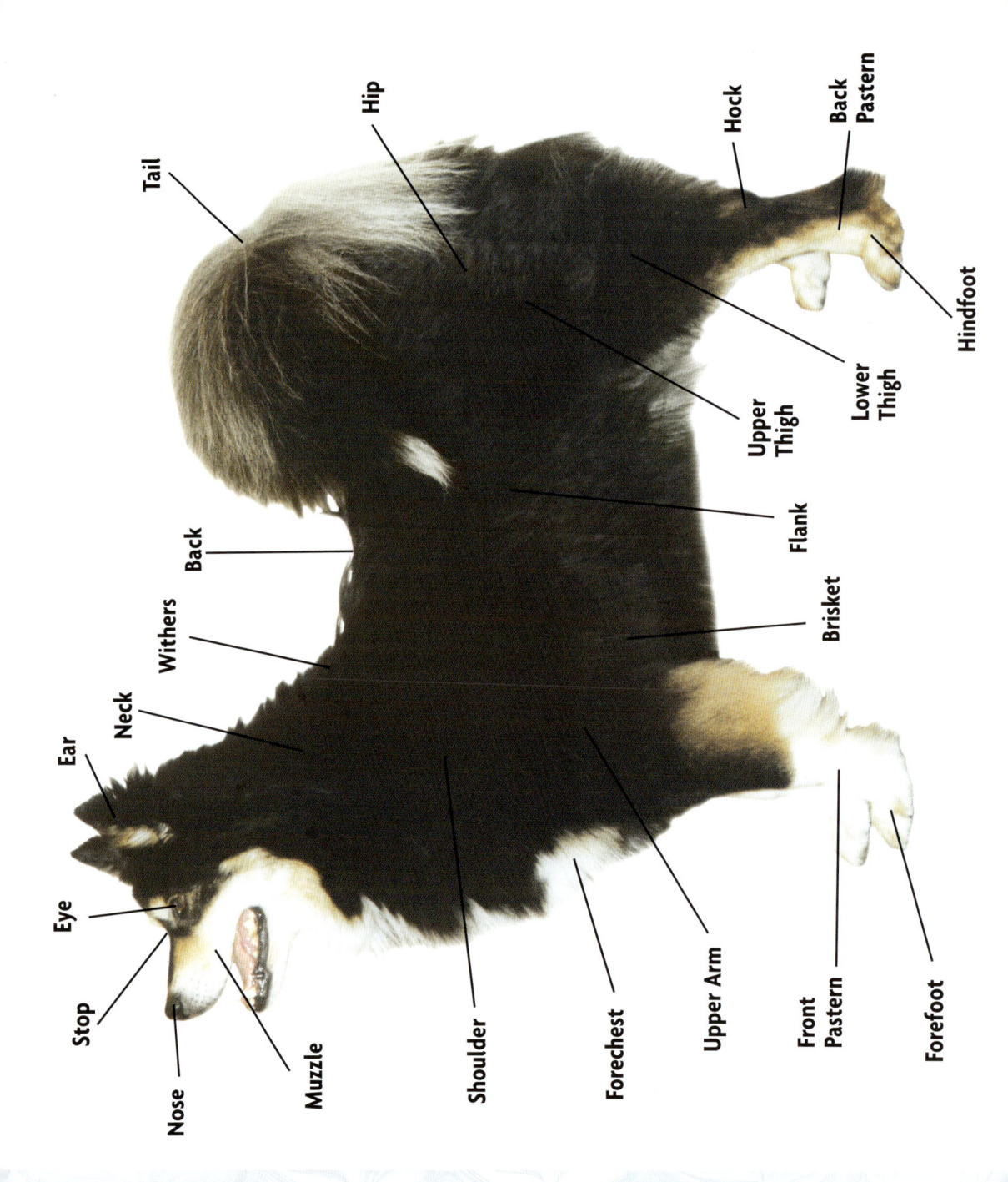

PHYSICAL STRUCTURE OF THE FINNISH LAPPHUND

HEALTH CARE OF YOUR
FINNISH LAPPHUND

Dogs suffer from many of the same physical illnesses as people and might even share many of the same psychological problems. Since people usually know more about human diseases than canine maladies, many of the terms used in this chapter will be familiar but not necessarily those used by vets. For example, we will use the familiar term *x-ray* instead of *radiograph*. We will also use the familiar term *symptoms*, even though dogs don't have symptoms, which are verbal descriptions of something the patient feels or observes himself that he regards as abnormal. Dogs have *clinical signs* since they cannot speak, so we have to look for these clinical signs...but we still use the term *symptoms* in the book.

Medicine is a constantly changing art, with some scientific input as well. Things alter as we learn more and more about basic sciences such as genetics and biochemistry, and have use of more sophisticated imaging techniques like Computer Aided Tomography (CAT scans) or Magnetic Resonance Imaging (MRI scans). There is academic dispute about many canine maladies, so different vets treat them in different ways, and some vets place a greater emphasis on surgical techniques than others.

SELECTING A VET
Your selection of a vet should be based on personal recommendation for his skills with small animals, especially dogs, and, if possible, spitz breeds. If the vet is based nearby, it will be helpful because you might have an emergency or need to make multiple visits for treatments.

All vets are licenced, and the main veterinary practice deals with routine medical issues such as infections, injuries and the promotion of health (for example, by vaccination). If the problem affecting your dog is more complex, your vet will refer your pet to someone with a more detailed knowledge of what is wrong. This will usually be a specialist at the nearest university veterinary school who is a veterinary dermatologist, veterinary ophthalmologist, etc; whatever is the relevant field.

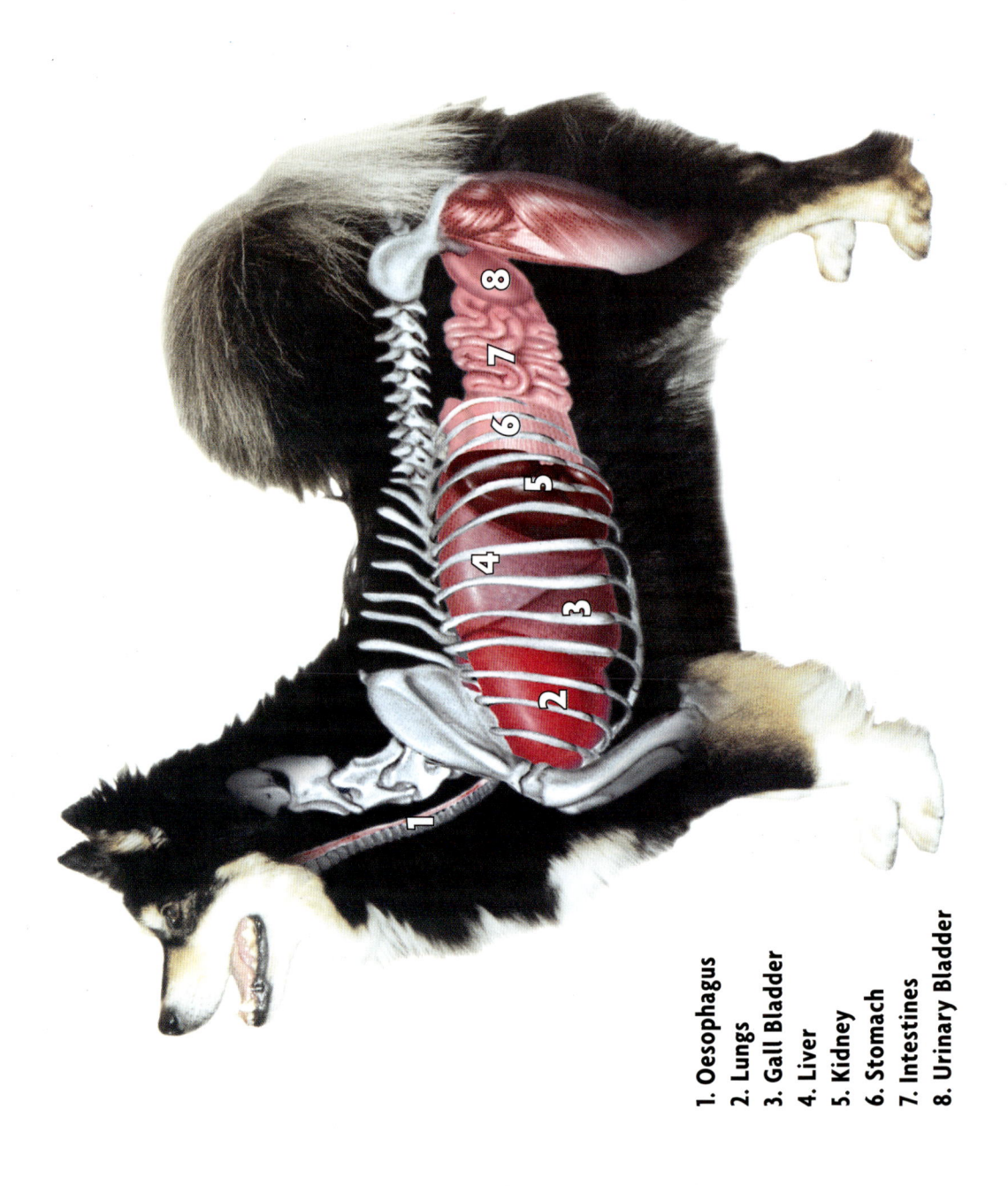

1. Oesophagus
2. Lungs
3. Gall Bladder
4. Liver
5. Kidney
6. Stomach
7. Intestines
8. Urinary Bladder

INTERNAL ORGANS OF THE FINNISH LAPPHUND

Health Care

Veterinary procedures are very costly and as the treatments available improve, they become more expensive. It is quite acceptable to discuss matters of cost with your vet; if there is more than one treatment option, cost may be a factor in deciding which route to take.

Insurance against veterinary cost is also becoming very popular. This may not pay for routine vaccinations, but will cover the costs for unexpected emergencies such as emergency surgery after a road-traffic accident. Some agencies offer special policies that cover exams, inoculations, teeth scaling and more, though these are quite costly.

PREVENTATIVE MEDICINE

It is much easier, less costly and more effective to practise preventative medicine than to fight bouts of illness and disease. Properly bred puppies of all breeds come from parents that were selected based upon their genetic disease profiles. The puppies' mother should have been vaccinated, free of all internal and external parasites and properly nourished. For these reasons, a visit to the vet who cared for the dam is recommended if at all possible. The dam passes disease resistance to her puppies, which should last from eight to ten weeks.

Unfortunately, she can also pass on parasites and infection.

Breakdown of Veterinary Income by Category

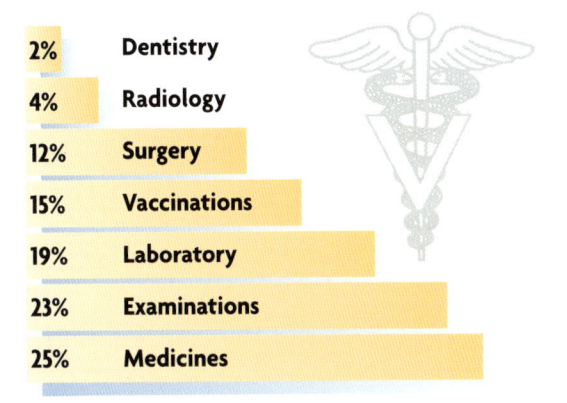

2%	Dentistry
4%	Radiology
12%	Surgery
15%	Vaccinations
19%	Laboratory
23%	Examinations
25%	Medicines

This is why knowledge about her health is useful in learning more about the health of the puppies.

A typical vet's income, categorised according to services performed. This survey dealt with small-animal (pets) practices.

WEANING TO FIVE MONTHS OLD

Puppies should be weaned by the time they are two months old. A puppy that remains for at least eight weeks with his mother and littermates usually adapts better to other dogs and people later in his life.

Sometimes new owners have their puppy examined by a vet immediately, which is a good idea unless the puppy is overtired by a long journey, in which case an appointment should be set up for the next day.

The puppy will have his teeth examined and have his skeletal conformation and general health checked prior to certification by the vet. Puppies in certain breeds have problems with their knee-

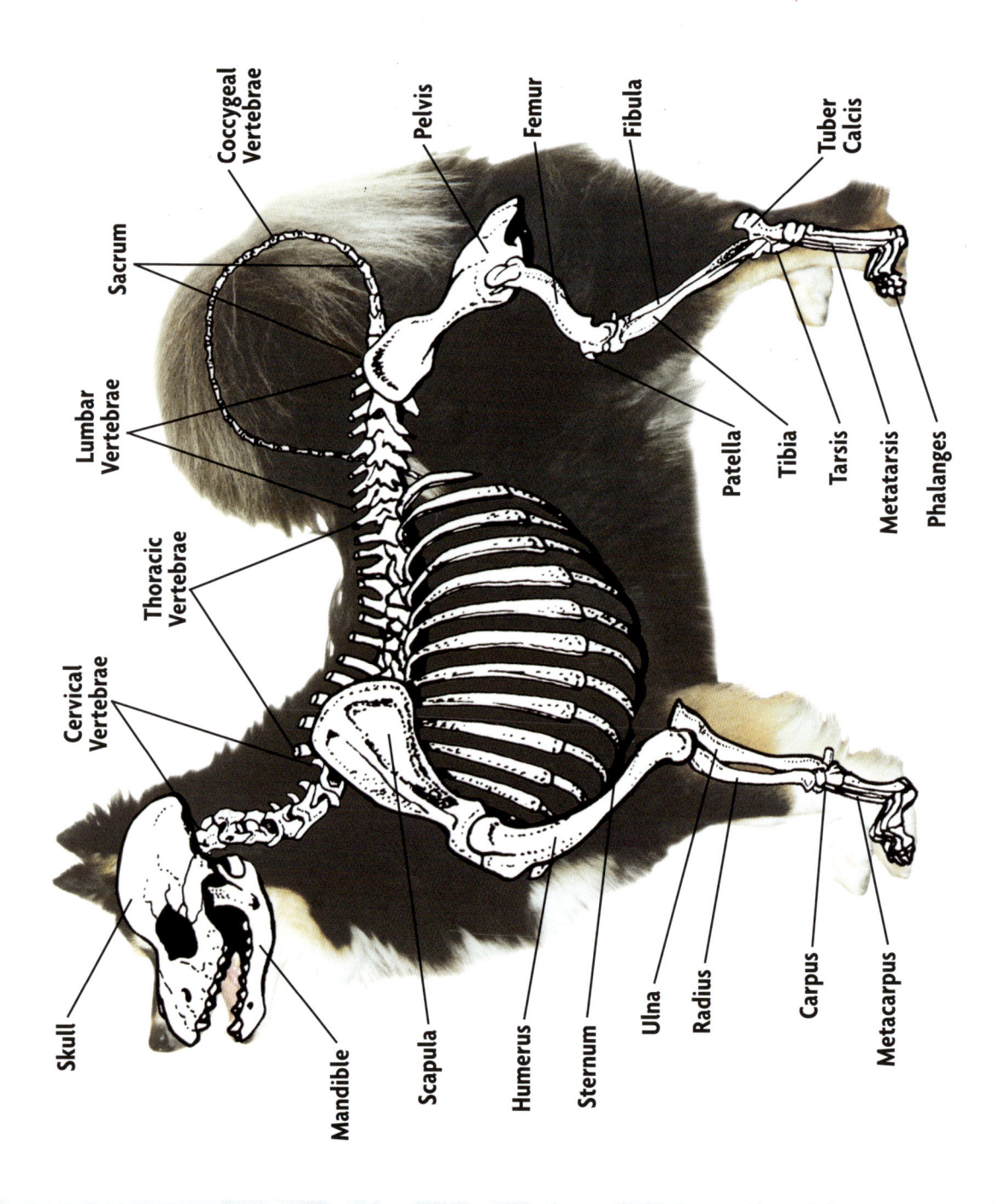

SKELETAL STRUCTURE OF THE FINNISH LAPPHUND

Health Care

> **MORE THAN VACCINES**
> Vaccinations help prevent your new puppy from contracting diseases, but they do not cure them. Proper nutrition as well as parasite control keep your dog healthy and less susceptible to many dangerous diseases. Remember that your dog depends on you to ensure his well-being.

caps, cataracts and other eye problems, heart murmurs and undescended testicles. They may also have personality problems and your vet might have training in temperament evaluation. Also at the first visit, the vet will set up a schedule for your pup's vaccinations.

VACCINATIONS

Most vaccinations are given by injection and should only be given by a vet. Both he and you should keep a record of the date of the injection, the identification of the vaccine and the amount given. Some vets give a first vaccination at eight weeks, but most dog breeders prefer the course not to commence until about ten weeks because of the risk of interaction with the antibodies produced by the mother. The

HEALTH AND VACCINATION TIMETABLE

AGE IN WEEKS:	6TH	8TH	10TH	12TH	14TH	16TH	20-24TH	52ND
Worm Control	✔	✔	✔	✔	✔	✔	✔	
Neutering								✔
Heartworm*		✔		✔		✔	✔	
Parvovirus	✔		✔		✔		✔	✔
Distemper		✔		✔		✔		✔
Hepatitis		✔		✔		✔		✔
Leptospirosis								✔
Parainfluenza	✔		✔		✔			✔
Dental Examination		✔					✔	✔
Complete Physical		✔					✔	✔
Coronavirus				✔			✔	✔
Kennel Cough	✔							
Hip Dysplasia								✔
Rabies*							✔	

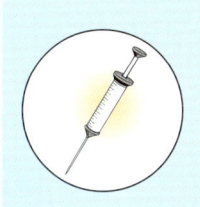

Vaccinations are not instantly effective. It takes about two weeks for the dog's immune system to develop antibodies. Most vaccinations require annual booster shots. Your vet should guide you in this regard.
*Not applicable in United Kingdom.

First Aid at a Glance

Burns
Place the affected area under cool water; use ice if only a small area is burnt.

Insect bites
Apply ice to relieve swelling; antihistamine dosed properly.

Animal bites
Clean any bleeding area; apply pressure until bleeding subsides; go to the vet.

Spider bites
Use cold compress and a pressurised pack to inhibit venom's spreading.

Antifreeze poisoning
Induce vomiting with hydrogen peroxide. Seek *immediate* veterinary help!

Fish hooks
Removal best handled by vet; hook must be cut in order to remove.

Snake bites
Pack ice around bite; contact vet quickly; identify snake for proper antivenin.

Road-traffic accident
Move dog from roadway with blanket; seek veterinary aid.

Shock
Calm the dog, keep him warm; seek immediate veterinary help.

Nosebleed
Apply cold compress to the nose; apply pressure to any visible abrasion.

Bleeding
Apply pressure above the area; treat wound by applying a cotton pack.

Heat stroke
Submerge dog in cold bath; cool down with fresh air and water; go to the vet.

Frostbite/Hypothermia
Warm the dog with a warm bath, electric blankets or hot water bottles.

Abrasions
Clean the wound and wash out thoroughly with fresh water; apply antiseptic.

‼ *Remember: an injured dog may attempt to bite an helping hand from fear and confusion. Always muzzle the dog before trying to offer assistance.* **‼**

vaccination timetable is usually based on a 15-day cycle. You must take your vet's advice as to when to vaccinate, as this may differ according to the vaccine used.

The usual vaccines contain immunising doses of several different viruses such as distemper, parvovirus, parainfluenza and hepatitis. There are other vaccines available when the puppy is at risk. You should rely upon professional advice. This is especially true for the booster immunisations. Most vaccination programmes require a booster when the puppy is a year old and once a year thereafter. In some cases, circumstances may require more or less frequent immunisations.

Kennel cough, more formally known as tracheobronchitis, is immunised against with a vaccine that is sprayed into the dog's nostrils. Kennel cough is usually included in routine vaccination, but it is often not as effective as the vaccines for other major diseases.

FIVE MONTHS TO ONE YEAR OF AGE
Unless you intend to breed or show your dog, neutering the

DISEASE REFERENCE CHART

	What is it?	What causes it?	Symptoms
Leptospirosis	Severe disease that affects the internal organs; can be spread to people.	A bacterium, which is often carried by rodents, that enters through mucous membranes and spreads quickly throughout the body.	Range from fever, vomiting and loss of appetite in less severe cases to shock, irreversible kidney damage and possibly death in most severe cases.
Rabies	Potentially deadly virus that infects warm-blooded mammals. Not seen in United Kingdom.	Bite from a carrier of the virus, mainly wild animals.	1st stage: dog exhibits change in behaviour, fear. 2nd stage: dog's behaviour becomes more aggressive. 3rd stage: loss of coordination, trouble with bodily functions.
Parvovirus	Highly contagious virus, potentially deadly.	Ingestion of the virus, which is usually spread through the faeces of infected dogs.	Most common: severe diarrhoea. Also vomiting, fatigue, lack of appetite.
Kennel cough	Contagious respiratory infection.	Combination of types of bacteria and virus. Most common: *Bordetella bronchiseptica* bacteria and parainfluenza virus.	Chronic cough.
Distemper	Disease primarily affecting respiratory and nervous system.	Virus that is related to the human measles virus.	Mild symptoms such as fever, lack of appetite and mucous secretion progress to evidence of brain damage, 'hard pad.'
Hepatitis	Virus primarily affecting the liver.	Canine adenovirus type I (CAV-1). Enters system when dog breathes in particles.	Lesser symptoms include listlessness, diarrhoea, vomiting. More severe symptoms include 'blue-eye' (clumps of virus in eye).
Coronavirus	Virus resulting in digestive problems.	Virus is spread through infected dog's faeces.	Stomach upset evidenced by lack of appetite, vomiting, diarrhoea.

FINNISH LAPPHUND

The Finnish Lapphund is a hardy, long-lived breed, with lively 16-year-olds not uncommon! This vibrant veteran is Multi Ch Lecibsin Catiano.

puppy at the appropriate age is recommended. Discuss this with your vet. Neutering/spaying has proven to be extremely beneficial to male and female dogs, respectively. Besides eliminating the possibility of pregnancy, it inhibits (but does not prevent) breast cancer in bitches and prostate cancer in male dogs. Discuss with your vet the best age at which to have your Lapphund neutered or spayed.

Your vet should provide your puppy with a thorough dental evaluation at six months of age, ascertaining whether all of the permanent teeth have erupted properly. A home dental-care regimen should be initiated at six months, including brushing weekly and providing good dental devices (such as hard rubber or nylon bones). Regular dental care promotes healthy teeth, fresh breath and a longer life for your dog.

DOGS OLDER THAN ONE YEAR
Continue to visit the vet at least once a year. There is no such disease as 'old age,' but bodily functions do change with age. The eyes and ears are no longer as efficient. Liver, kidney and intestinal functions often decline. Proper dietary changes, recommended by your vet, can make life more pleasant for your ageing Finnish Lapphund and you.

SKIN PROBLEMS
Vets are consulted by dog owners for skin problems more than for any other group of diseases or maladies. A dog's skin is as sensitive, if not more so, than human skin, and both suffer from almost the same ailments (though the occurrence of acne in most breeds is rare!). For this reason, veterinary dermatology has developed into a speciality practised by many vets.

Since many skin problems have visual symptoms that are almost identical, it requires the skill of an experienced veterinary dermatologist to identify and cure many of the more severe skin disorders. Pet shops sell many treatments for skin problems, but most of the treatments are directed at symptoms and not at the underlying problem(s). If your dog is suffering from a skin disorder, you should seek professional assistance as quickly as possible. As with all diseases, the earlier a problem is identified and treated, the more likely it is that the cure will be successful.

HEREDITARY SKIN DISORDERS

Veterinary dermatologists are currently researching a number of skin disorders that are believed to have a hereditary basis. These inherited diseases are transmitted by both parents, who appear (phenotypically) normal but have a recessive gene for the disease, meaning that they carry, but are not affected by, the disease. These diseases pose serious problems to breeders because in some instances there are no methods of identifying carriers. Often the secondary diseases associated with these skin conditions are even more debilitating than the skin disorders themselves, including cancers and respiratory problems.

Among the hereditary skin disorders, for which the mode of inheritance is known, are acrodermatitis, cutaneous asthenia (Ehlers-Danlos syndrome), sebaceous adenitis, cyclic hematopoiesis, dermatomyositis, IgA deficiency, colour dilution alopaecia and nodular dermatofibrosis. Some of these disorders are limited to one or two breeds, while others affect a large number of breeds. All inherited diseases must be diagnosed and treated by a veterinary specialist.

PARASITE BITES

Many of us are allergic to insect bites. The bites itch, erupt and may even become infected. Dogs have the same reaction to fleas, ticks and/or mites. When an insect lands on you, you have the chance to whisk it away with your hand. Unfortunately, when a dog is bitten by a flea, tick or mite, it can only scratch it away or bite it. By the time the dog has been bitten, the parasite has done some of its damage. It may also have laid eggs, which will cause further problems in the near future. The itching from parasite bites is probably due to the saliva injected into the site when the parasite sucks the dog's blood.

AIRBORNE ALLERGIES

Just as humans suffer from hay fever during the pollinating season, many dogs suffer from the same allergies. When the pollen count is high, your dog might suffer but don't expect him to sneeze and have a runny nose as a human would. Dogs react to pollen allergies in the same way they react to fleas—they scratch and bite themselves. Dogs, like humans, can be tested for allergens. Discuss the testing with your vet.

AUTO-IMMUNE ILLNESSES

An auto-immune illness is one in which the immune system overacts and does not recognise parts

Food problems often are difficult to diagnose, as the symptoms don't always specifically point to food as the cause. If you suspect a diet-related problem, consult with your vet about changing your dog's food to ensure that he continues to receive proper nutrition.

of the affected person; rather, the immune system starts to react as if these parts were foreign and need to be destroyed. An example is rheumatoid arthritis, which occurs when the body does not recognise the joints, thus leading to a very painful and damaging reaction in the joints. This has nothing to do with age, so can occur in children. The wear-and-tear arthritis of the older person or dog is osteoarthritis.

Lupus is an auto-immune disease that affects dogs as well as people. It can take variable forms, affecting the kidneys, bones and the skin. It can be fatal, so is treated with steroids, which can themselves have very significant side effects. The steroids calm down the allergic reaction to the body's tissues, which helps the lupus, but the steroids also decrease the body's reaction to real foreign substances such as bacteria, and they also thin the skin and bones.

FOOD PROBLEMS

FOOD ALLERGIES

Some dogs can be allergic to many foods that are best-sellers and highly recommended by breeders and vets. Changing the brand of food that you buy may not eliminate the problem if the element to which the dog is allergic is contained in the new brand.

Recognising a food allergy in a dog can be difficult. Humans often have rashes when they eat foods to which they are allergic, or have swelling of the lips or eyes. Dogs do not usually develop rashes, but react in the same way as they do to an airborne or bite allergy—they itch, scratch and bite. While pollen allergies are usually seasonal, food allergies are year-round problems.

Diagnosis of food allergy is based on a two- to four-week dietary trial with a home-cooked diet fed to the exclusion of all other foods. The diet should consist of boiled rice or potato with a source of protein that the dog has never eaten before, such as fresh or frozen fish, lamb or even something as exotic as

DENTAL HEALTH

A dental examination is in order when the dog is between six months and one year of age so that any permanent teeth that have erupted incorrectly can be corrected. It is important to begin a brushing routine at home, using a toothbrush made for dogs and a specially formulated canine toothpaste. Durable nylon and safe edible chews should be a part of your Lapphund's arsenal for good health, good teeth and pleasant breath. The vast majority of dogs three to four years old and older has diseases of the gums from lack of dental attention. Using the various types of dental chews can be very effective in controlling dental plaque.

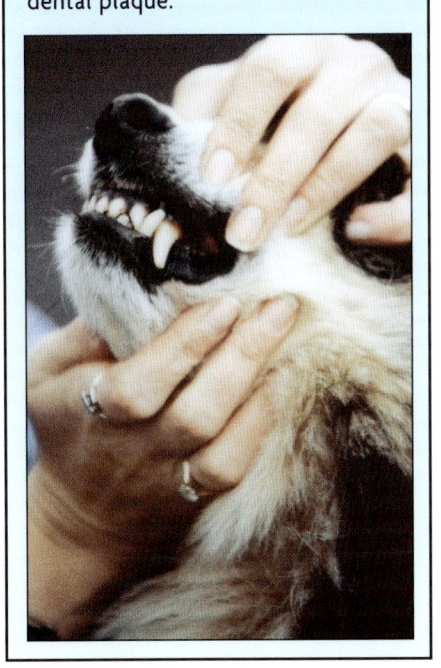

pheasant. Water has to be the only drink, and it is really important that no other foods are fed during this trial.

If the dog's condition improves, you will need to try the original diet once again to see if the itching resumes. If it does, then this confirms the diagnosis that the dog is allergic to his original diet. The treatment is long-term feeding of something that does not distress the dog's skin, which may be in the form of one of the commercially available hypoallergenic diets or the homemade diet that you created for the allergy trial.

FOOD INTOLERANCE

Food intolerance is the inability of the dog to completely digest certain foods. This occurs because the dog does not have the chemicals necessary to digest some foodstuffs. These chemicals are called enzymes. All puppies have the enzymes necessary to digest canine milk, but some dogs do not have the enzymes to digest a very different form of milk that is commonly found in human households—milk from cows. In such dogs, drinking cows' milk results in loose bowels, stomach pains and the passage of gas.

Dogs often do not have the enzymes to digest soy or other beans. The treatment is to exclude the foodstuffs that upset your Finnish Lapphund's digestion.

A male dog flea, *Ctenocephalides canis*.

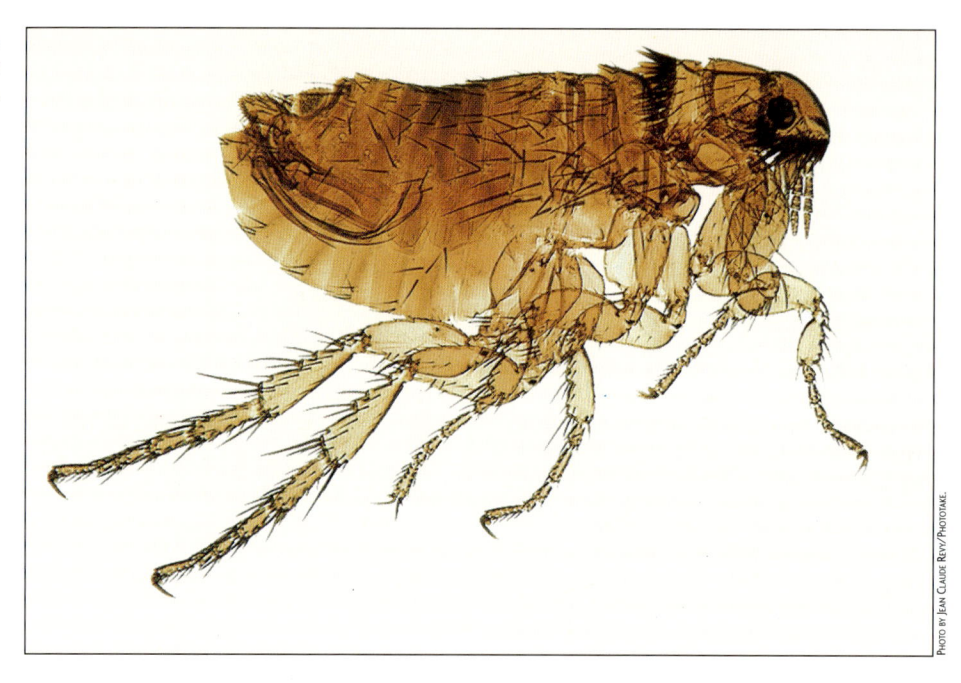

EXTERNAL PARASITES

FLEAS
Of all the problems to which dogs are prone, none is more well known and frustrating than fleas. Flea infestation is relatively simple to cure but difficult to prevent. Parasites that are harboured inside the body are a bit more difficult to eradicate but they are easier to control.

To control flea infestation, you have to understand the flea's life cycle. Fleas are often thought of as a summertime problem, but centrally heated homes have changed the patterns and fleas can be found at any time of the year. The most effective method of flea control is a two-stage approach: one stage to kill the adult fleas, and the other to control the development of pre-adult fleas. Unfortunately, no single active ingredient is effective against all stages of the life cycle.

> **FLEA KILLER CAUTION—'POISON'**
> Flea-killers are poisonous. You should not spray these toxic chemicals on areas of a dog's body that he licks, including his genitals and his face. Flea killers taken internally are a better answer, but check with your vet in case internal therapy is not advised for your dog.

Life Cycle Stages

During its life, a flea will pass through four life stages: egg, larva, pupa or nymph and adult. The adult stage is the most visible and irritating stage of the flea life cycle, and this is why the majority of flea-control products concentrate on this stage. The fact is that adult fleas account for only 1% of the total flea population, and the other 99% exist in pre-adult stages, i.e. eggs, larvae and nymphs. The pre-adult stages are barely visible to the naked eye.

The Life Cycle of the Flea

Eggs are laid on the dog, usually in quantities of about 20 or 30, several times a day. The adult female flea must have a blood meal before each egg-laying session. When first laid, the eggs will cling to the dog's hair, as the eggs are still moist. However, they will quickly dry out and fall from the dog, especially if the dog moves around or scratches. Many eggs will fall off in the dog's favourite area or an area in which he spends a lot of time, such as his bed.

Once the eggs fall from the dog onto the carpet or furniture, they will hatch into larvae. This takes from one to ten days. Larvae are not particularly mobile and will usually travel only a few inches from where they hatch. However, they do have a tendency to move away from bright light and heavy traffic—under furniture and behind doors are common places to find high quantities of flea larvae.

The flea larvae feed on dead organic matter, including adult flea faeces, until they are ready to change into adult fleas. Fleas will usually remain as larvae for around seven days. After this period, the larvae will pupate into protective pupae. While inside the pupae, the larvae will undergo

> ### EN GARDE: CATCHING FLEAS OFF GUARD!
> Consider the following ways to arm yourself against fleas:
> - Add a small amount of pennyroyal or eucalyptus oil to your dog's bath. These natural remedies repel fleas.
> - Supplement your dog's food with fresh garlic (minced or grated) and an hearty amount of brewer's yeast, both of which ward off fleas.
> - Use a flea comb on your dog daily. Submerge fleas in a cup of bleach to kill them quickly.
> - Confine the dog to only a few rooms to limit the spread of fleas in the home.
> - Vacuum daily...and get all of the crevices! Dispose of the bag every few days until the problem is under control.
> - Wash your dog's bedding daily. Cover cushions where your dog sleeps with towels, and wash the towels often.

Fleas have been measured as being able to jump 300,000 times and can jump 150 times their length in any direction, including straight up.

metamorphosis and change into adult fleas. This can take as little time as a few days, but the adult fleas can remain inside the pupae waiting to hatch for up to two years. The pupae are signaled to hatch by certain stimuli, such as physical pressure—the pupae's being stepped on, heat from an animal's lying on the pupae or increased carbon-dioxide levels and vibrations—indicating that a suitable host is available.

Once hatched, the adult flea must feed within a few days. Once the adult flea finds an host, it will not leave voluntarily. It only becomes dislodged by grooming or the host animal's scratching. The adult flea will remain on the host for the duration of its life unless forcibly removed.

A scanning electron micrograph of a dog or cat flea, *Ctenocephalides*, magnified more than 100x. This image has been colorized for effect.

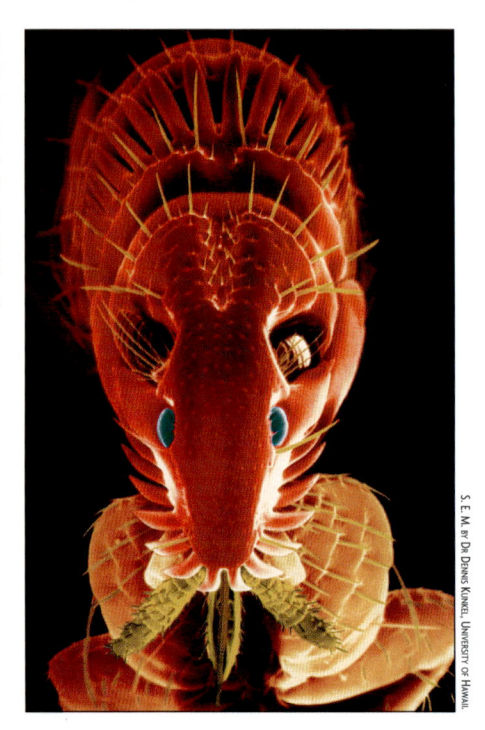

TREATING THE ENVIRONMENT AND THE DOG

Treating fleas should be a two-pronged attack. First, the environment needs to be treated; this includes carpets and furniture, especially the dog's bedding and areas underneath furniture. The environment should be treated with a household spray containing an Insect Growth Regulator (IGR) and an insecticide to kill the adult fleas. Most IGRs are effective against eggs and larvae; they actually mimic the fleas' own hormones and stop the eggs and larvae from developing into adult fleas. There are currently no treatments available to attack the pupa stage of the life cycle, so the adult insecticide is used to kill the newly hatched adult fleas before they find a host. Most IGRs are active for many months, while

THE LIFE CYCLE OF THE FLEA

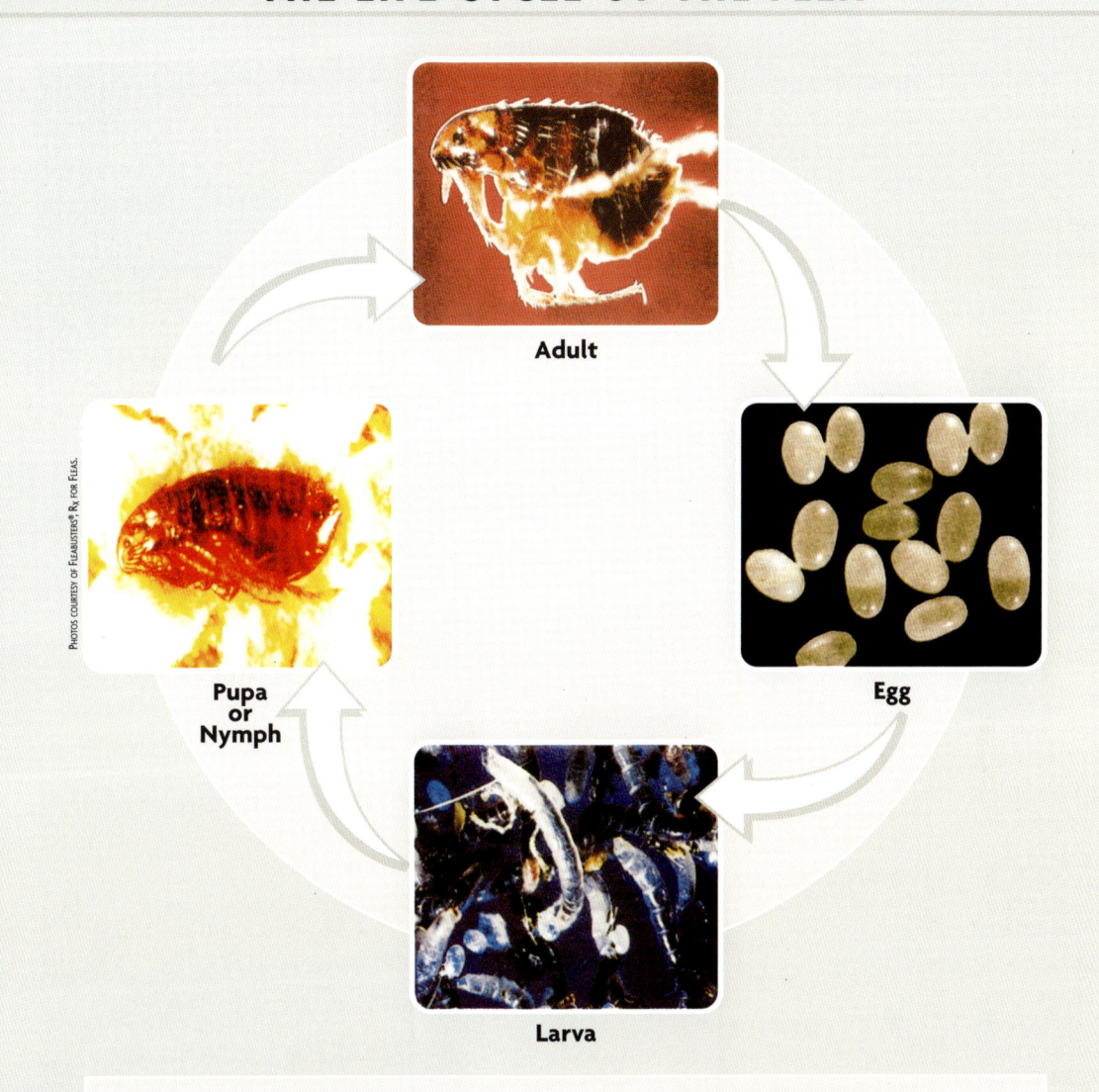

Adult

Egg

Larva

Pupa or Nymph

Fleas have been around for millions of years and have adapted to changing host animals. They are able to go through a complete life cycle in less than one month or they can extend their lives to almost two years by remaining as pupae or cocoons. They do not need blood or any other food for up to 20 months.

INSECT GROWTH REGULATOR (IGR)

Two types of products should be used when treating fleas—a product to treat the pet and a product to treat the home. Adult fleas represent less than 1% of the flea population. The pre-adult fleas (eggs, larvae and pupae) represent more than 99% of the flea population and are found in the environment; it is in the case of pre-adult fleas that products containing an Insect Growth Regulator (IGR) should be used in the home.

IGRs are a new class of compounds used to prevent the development of insects. They do not kill the insect outright, but instead use the insect's biology against it to stop it from completing its growth. Products that contain methoprene are the world's first and leading IGRs. Used to control fleas and other insects, this type of IGR will stop flea larvae from developing and protect the house for up to seven months.

The American dog tick, *Dermacentor variabilis*, is probably the most common tick found on dogs. Look at the strength in its eight legs! No wonder it's hard to detach them.

adult insecticides are only active for a few days.

When treating with an household spray, it is a good idea to vacuum before applying the product. This stimulates as many pupae as possible to hatch into adult fleas. The vacuum cleaner should also be treated with an insecticide to prevent the eggs and larvae that have been collected into the vacuum bag from hatching.

The second stage of treatment is to apply an adult insecticide to the dog. Traditionally, this would be in the form of a collar or a spray, but more recent innovations include digestible insecticides that poison the fleas when they ingest the dog's blood. Alternatively, there are drops that, when placed on the back of the dog's neck, spread throughout the hair and skin to kill adult fleas.

TICKS

Though not as common as fleas, ticks are found all over the tropical and temperate world. They don't bite, like fleas; they harpoon. They dig their sharp proboscis (nose) into the dog's

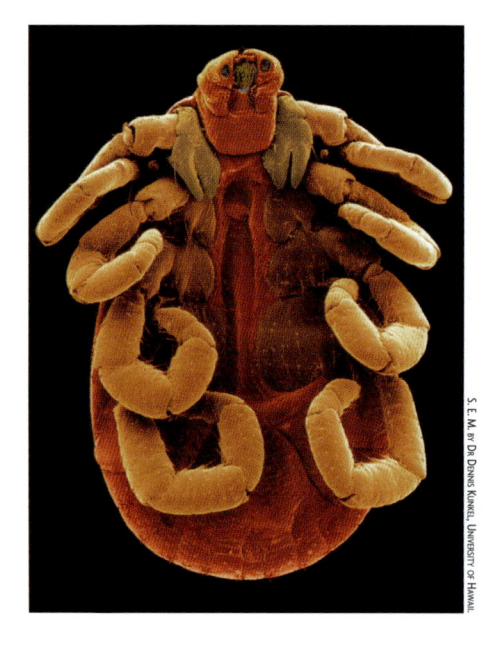

S. E. M. BY DR. DENNIS KUNKEL, UNIVERSITY OF HAWAII

Health Care

skin and drink the blood. Their only food and drink is dog's blood. Dogs can get Lyme disease, Rocky Mountain spotted fever (usually in the US only), tick bite paralysis and many other diseases from ticks. They may live where fleas are found and they like to hide in cracks or seams in walls. They are controlled the same way fleas are controlled.

The American dog tick, *Dermacentor variabilis*, may well be the most common dog tick in many geographical areas, especially those areas where the climate is hot and humid. Most dog ticks have life expectancies of a week to six months, depending upon climatic conditions. They can neither jump nor fly, but they can crawl slowly and can range up to 5 metres (16 feet) to reach a sleeping or unsuspecting dog.

MITES

Just as fleas and ticks can be problematic for your dog, mites can also lead to an itchy nuisance. Microscopic in size, mites are related to ticks and generally take up permanent residence on their host animal—in this case, your dog! The term *mange* refers to any infestation caused by one of the mighty mites, of which there are six varieties that concern dog owners.

DEER-TICK CROSSING

The great outdoors may be fun for your dog, but it also is an home to dangerous ticks. Deer ticks carry a bacterium known as *Borrelia burgdorferi* and are most active in the autumn and spring. When infections are caught early, penicillin and tetracycline are effective antibiotics, but if left untreated the bacteria may cause neurological, kidney and cardiac problems as well as long-term trouble with walking and painful joints.

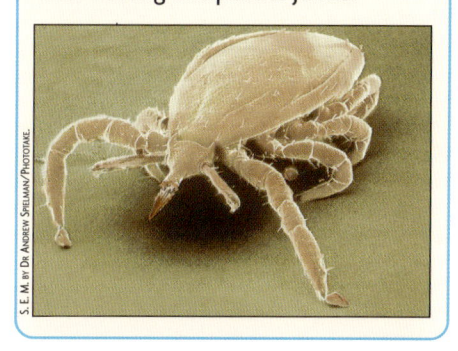

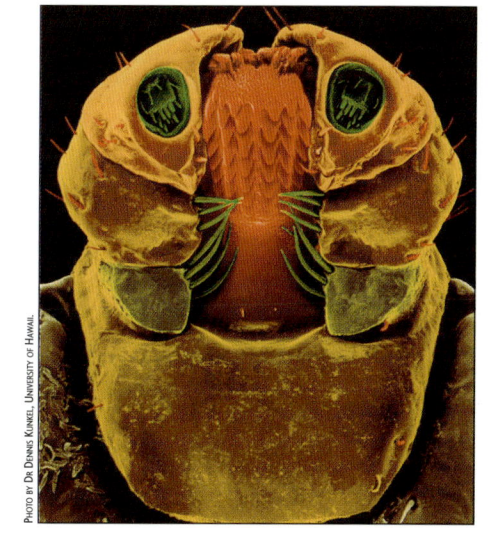

The head of an American dog tick, *Dermacentor variabilis*, enlarged and colorized for effect.

144 FINNISH LAPPHUND

The mange mite, *Psoroptes bovis*, can infest cattle and other domestic animals.

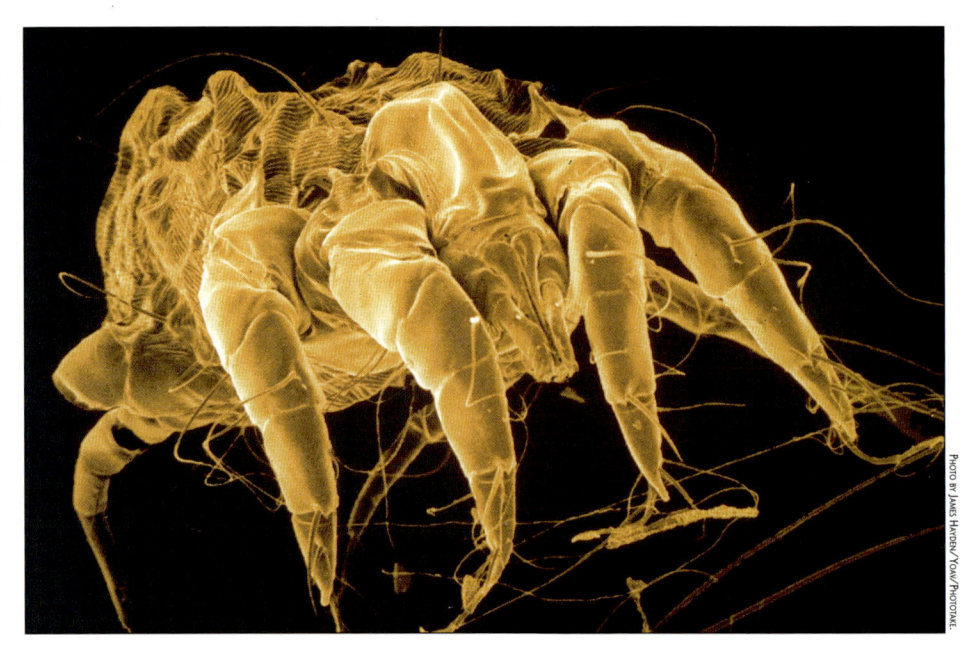

Photo by James Hayden/Yoav/Phototake

Human lice look like dog lice; the two are closely related.
Photo by Dwight R Kuhn.

Demodex mites cause a condition known as demodicosis (sometimes called red mange or follicular mange), in which the mites live in the dog's hair follicles and sebaceous glands. This type of mange is commonly passed from the dam to her puppies and usually shows up on the puppies' muzzles, though demodicosis is not transferable from one normal dog to another. Most dogs recover from this type of mange without any treatment, though topical therapies are commonly prescribed by the vet.

The *Cheyletiellosis* mite is the hook-mouthed culprit associated with 'walking dandruff,' a condition that affects dogs as well as cats and rabbits. This mite lives on the surface of the animal's skin and is readily transferable through direct or indirect contact with an affected animal. The dandruff is present in the form of scaly skin, which may or may not be itchy. If not treated, this mange can affect a whole kennel of dogs and can be spread to humans as well.

The *Sarcoptes* mite causes intense itching on the dog in the form of a condition known as scabies or sarcoptic mange. The cycle of the *Sarcoptes* mite lasts about three weeks, and the mites live in the top layer of the dog's

Health Care

skin (epidermis), preferably in areas with little hair. Scabies is highly contagious and can be passed to humans. Sometimes an allergic reaction to the mite worsens the severe itching associated with sarcoptic mange.

Ear mites, *Otodectes cynotis*, lead to otodectic mange, which most commonly affects the outer ear canal of the dog, though other areas can be affected as well. Dogs with ear-mite infestation commonly scratch at their ears, causing further irritation, and shake their heads. Dark brown droppings in the outer ear confirm the diagnosis. Your vet can prescribe a treatment to flush out the ears and kill any eggs in the ears. A complete month of treatment is necessary to cure the mange.

Two other mites, less common in dogs, include *Dermanyssus gallinae* (the poultry or red mite) and *Eutrombicula alfreddugesi* (the North American mite associated with trombiculidiasis or chigger infestation). The poultry mite frequently lives on chickens, but can transfer to dogs who spend time near farm animals. Chigger infestation affects dogs who have exposure to woodlands. The types of mange caused by both of these mites are treatable by vets.

> **NOT A DROP TO DRINK**
> Never allow your dog to swim in polluted water or public areas where water quality can be suspect. Even perfectly clear water can harbour parasites, many of which can cause serious to fatal illnesses in canines. Areas inhabited by waterfowl and other wildlife are especially dangerous.

INTERNAL PARASITES

Most animals—fishes, birds and mammals, including dogs and humans—have worms and other parasites that live inside their bodies. According to Dr Herbert R Axelrod, the fish pathologist, there are two kinds of parasites: dumb and smart. The smart parasites live in peaceful cooperation with their hosts (symbiosis), while the dumb parasites kill their hosts. Most worm infections are relatively easy to control. If they are not controlled, they weaken the host dog to the point that other medical problems occur, but they do not kill the host as dumb parasites would.

> **DO NOT MIX**
> Never mix parasite control products without first consulting your vet. Some products can become toxic when combined with others and can cause fatal consequences.

A brown dog tick, *Rhipicephalus sanguineus*, is an uncommon but annoying tick found on dogs.
Photo by Carolina Biological Supply/Phototake.

The roundworm Rhabditis can infect both dogs and humans.

The roundworm, Ascaris lumbricoides.

ROUNDWORMS

Average-size dogs can pass 1,360,000 roundworm eggs every day. For example, if there were only 1 million dogs in the world, the world would be saturated with thousands of tons of dog faeces. These faeces would contain around 15,000,000,000 roundworm eggs.

Up to 31% of home yards and children's sand boxes in the US contain roundworm eggs.

Flushing dog's faeces down the toilet is not a safe practice because the usual sewage treatments do not destroy roundworm eggs.

Infected puppies start shedding roundworm eggs at three weeks of age. They can be infected by their mother's milk.

ROUNDWORMS

The roundworms that infect dogs are known scientifically as *Toxocara canis*. They live in the dog's intestines and shed eggs continually. It has been estimated that a dog produces about 6 or more ounces of faeces every day. Each ounce of faeces averages hundreds of thousands of roundworm eggs. There are no known areas in which dogs roam that do not contain roundworm eggs. The greatest danger of roundworms is that they infect people, too! It is wise to have your dog tested regularly for roundworms.

In young puppies, roundworms cause bloated bellies, diarrhoea, coughing and vomiting, and are transmitted from the dam (through blood or milk). Affected puppies will not appear as animated as normal puppies. The worms appear spaghetti-like, measuring as long as 15 cms (6 inches). Adult dogs can acquire roundworms through coprophagia (eating contaminated faeces) or by killing rodents that carry roundworms.

Roundworm infection can kill puppies and cause severe problems in adults, as the hatched larvae travel to the lungs and trachea through the bloodstream. Cleanliness is the best preventative for roundworms. Always pick up after your dog and dispose of faeces in appropriate receptacles.

Health Care

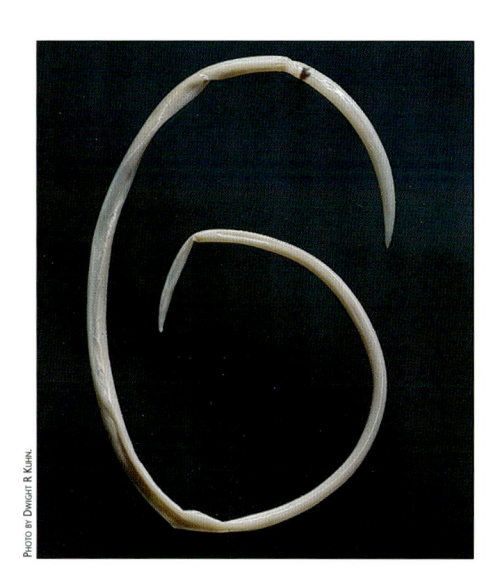

HOOKWORMS

In the United States, dog owners have to be concerned about four different species of hookworm, the most common and most serious of which is *Ancylostoma caninum*, which prefers warm climates. The others are *Ancylostoma braziliense*, *Ancylostoma tubaeforme* and *Uncinaria stenocephala*, the latter of which is a concern to dogs living in the Northern US and Canada, as this species prefers cold climates. Hookworms are dangerous to humans as well as to dogs and cats, and can be the cause of severe anemia due to iron deficiency. The worm uses its teeth to attach itself to the dog's intestines and changes the site of its attachment about six times per day. Each time the worm repositions itself, the dog loses blood and can become anemic. *Ancylostoma caninum* is the most likely of the four species to cause anemia in the dog.

Symptoms of hookworm infection include dark stools, weight loss, general weakness, pale coloration and anemia, as well as possible skin problems. Fortunately, hookworms are easily purged from the affected dog with a number of medications that have proven effective. Discuss these with your vet. Most heartworm preventatives include a hookworm insecticide as well.

Owners also must be aware that hookworms can infect humans, who can acquire the larvae through exposure to contaminated faeces. Since the worms cannot complete their life cycle on a human, the worms simply infest the skin and cause irritation. This condition is known as cutaneous larva migrans syndrome. As a preventative, use disposable gloves or a 'poop-scoop' to pick up your dog's droppings and prevent your dog (or neighbourhood cats) from defecating in children's play areas.

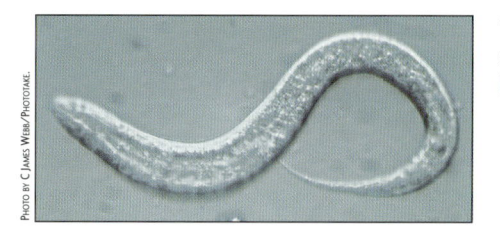

The hookworm, *Ancylostoma caninum*.

The infective stage of the hookworm larva.

TAPEWORMS

Humans, rats, squirrels, foxes, coyotes, wolves and domestic dogs are all susceptible to tapeworm infection. Except in humans, tapeworms are usually not a fatal infection. Infected individuals can harbor 1000 parasitic worms.

Tapeworms, like some other types of worm, are hermaphroditic, meaning male and female in the same worm.

If dogs eat infected rats or mice, or anything else injected with tapeworm, they get the tapeworm disease. One month after attaching to a dog's intestine, the worm starts shedding eggs. These eggs are infective immediately. Infective eggs can live for a few months without a host animal.

The head and rostellum (the round prominence on the scolex) of a tapeworm, which infects dogs and humans.

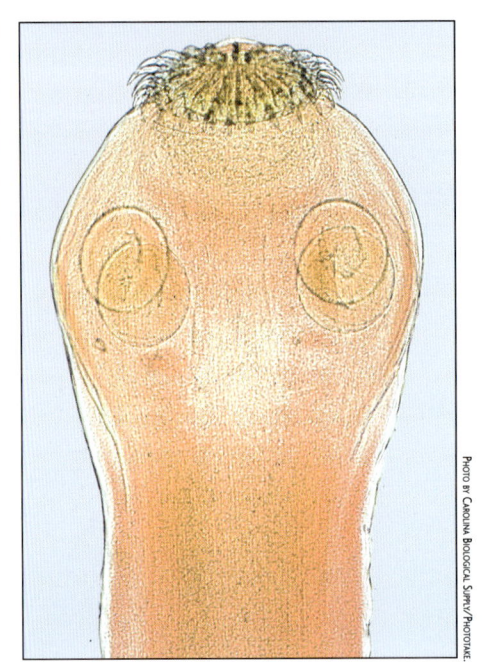

TAPEWORMS

There are many species of tapeworm, all of which are carried by fleas! The most common tapeworm affecting dogs is known as *Dipylidium caninum*. The dog eats the flea and starts the tapeworm cycle. Humans can also be infected with tapeworms—so don't eat fleas! Fleas are so small that your dog could pass them onto your hands, your plate or your food and thus make it possible for you to ingest a flea that is carrying tapeworm eggs.

While tapeworm infection is not life-threatening in dogs (smart parasite!), it can be the cause of a very serious liver disease for humans. About 50% of the humans infected with *Echinococcus multilocularis*, a type of tapeworm that causes alveolar hydatid, perish.

WHIPWORMS

In North America, whipworms are counted among the most common parasitic worms in dogs. The whipworm's scientific name is *Trichuris vulpis*. These worms attach themselves in the lower parts of the intestine, where they feed. Affected dogs may only experience upset tummies, colic and diarrhoea. These worms, however, can live for months or years in the dog, beginning their larval stage in the small intestine, spending their adult stage in the large intestine and finally passing

Health Care

infective eggs through the dog's faeces. The only way to detect whipworms is through a faecal examination, though this is not always foolproof. Treatment for whipworms is tricky, due to the worms' unusual life-cycle pattern, and very often dogs are reinfected due to exposure to infective eggs on the ground. The whipworm eggs can survive in the environment for as long as five years, thus cleaning up droppings in your own backyard as well as in public places is absolutely essential for sanitation purposes and the health of your dog.

THREADWORMS

Though less common than roundworms, hookworms and those listed above, threadworms concern dog owners in the Southwestern US and Gulf Coast area where the climate is hot and humid. Living in the small intestine of the dog, this worm measures a mere 2 millimetres and is round in shape. Like that of the whipworm, the threadworm's life cycle is very complex and the eggs and larvae are passed through the feces. A deadly disease in humans, *Strongyloides* readily infects people, and the handling of faeces is the most common means of transmission. Threadworms are most often seen in young puppies; bloody diarrhoea and pneumonia are symptoms. Sick puppies must be isolated and treated immediately; vets recommend a follow-up treatment one month later.

HEARTWORM PREVENTATIVES

There are many heartworm preventatives on the market, many of which are sold at your vet's office. These products can be given daily or monthly, depending on the manufacturer's instructions. All of these preventatives contain chemical insecticides directed at killing heartworms, which leads to some controversy among dog owners. In effect, heartworm preventatives are necessary evils, though you should determine how necessary based on your pet's lifestyle. There is no doubt that heartworm is a dreadful disease that threatens the life of dogs. However, the likelihood of your dog's being bitten by an infected mosquito is slim in most places, and a mosquito-repellent or a herbal remedy is much safer for your dog and will not compromise his immune system (the way heartworm preventatives will). Should you decide to use the traditional preventative 'medications,' you can consider giving the pill every other or third month. Since the toxins in the pill will kill the heartworms at all stages of development, the pill would be effective in killing larvae, nymphs or adults and it takes four months for the larvae to reach the adult stage. Thus, there is no rationale to poisoning the dog's system on a monthly basis. Lastly, do not give the pill during the winter months since there are no mosquitoes around to pass on their infection, unless you live in a tropical environment.

Life Cycle of the Heartworm

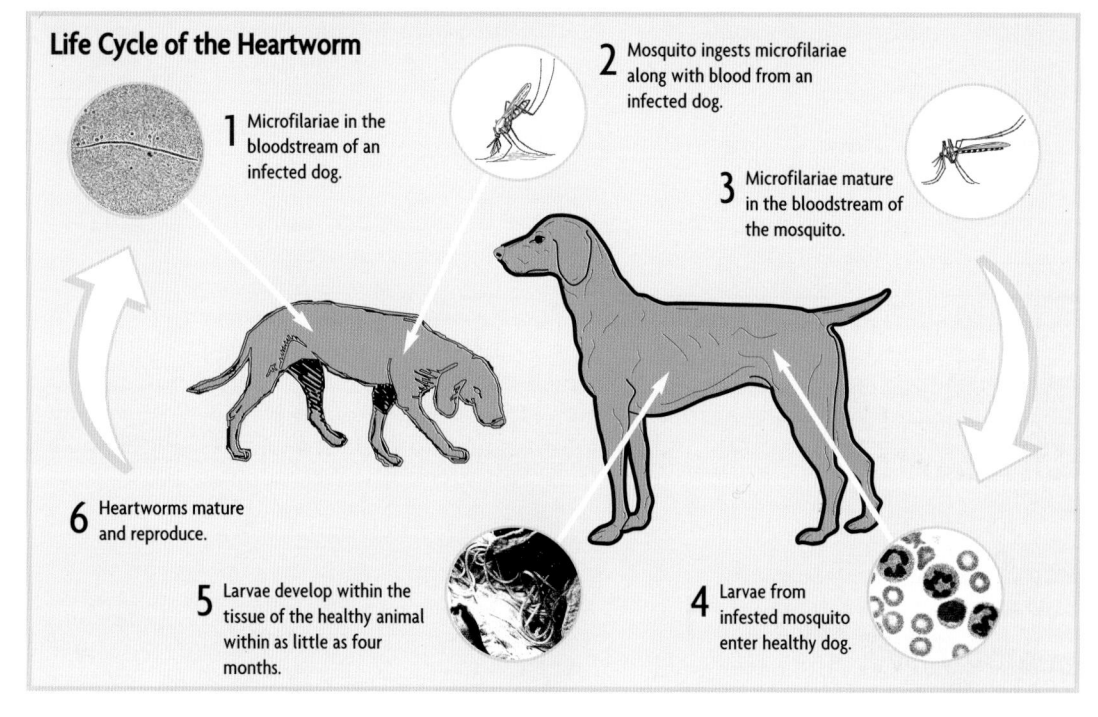

1. Microfilariae in the bloodstream of an infected dog.
2. Mosquito ingests microfilariae along with blood from an infected dog.
3. Microfilariae mature in the bloodstream of the mosquito.
4. Larvae from infested mosquito enter healthy dog.
5. Larvae develop within the tissue of the healthy animal within as little as four months.
6. Heartworms mature and reproduce.

HEARTWORMS

Heartworms are thin, extended worms up to 30 cms (12 inches) long, which live in a dog's heart and the major blood vessels surrounding it. Dogs may have up to 200 worms. Symptoms may be loss of energy, loss of appetite, coughing, the development of a pot belly and anemia.

Heartworms are transmitted by mosquitoes. The mosquito drinks the blood of an infected dog and takes in larvae with the blood. The larvae, called microfilariae, develop within the body of the mosquito and are passed on to the next dog bitten after the larvae mature. It takes two to three weeks for the larvae to develop to the infective stage within the body of the mosquito. Dogs are usually treated at about six weeks of age and maintained on a prophylactic dose given monthly.

Blood testing for heartworms is not necessarily indicative of how seriously your dog is infected. Although this is a dangerous disease of which US owners should be aware, it is not easy for a dog to be infected. Discuss the various preventatives with your vet, as there are many different types now available. Together you can decide on a safe course of prevention for your dog.

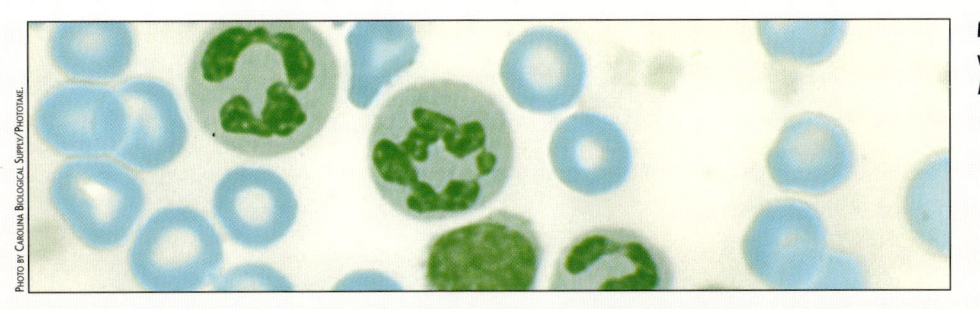

Magnified heartworm larvae, *Dirofilaria immitis.*

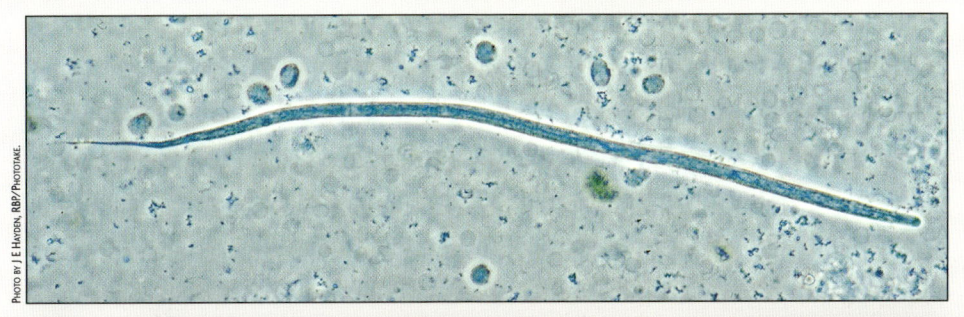

Heartworm, *Dirofilaria immitis.*

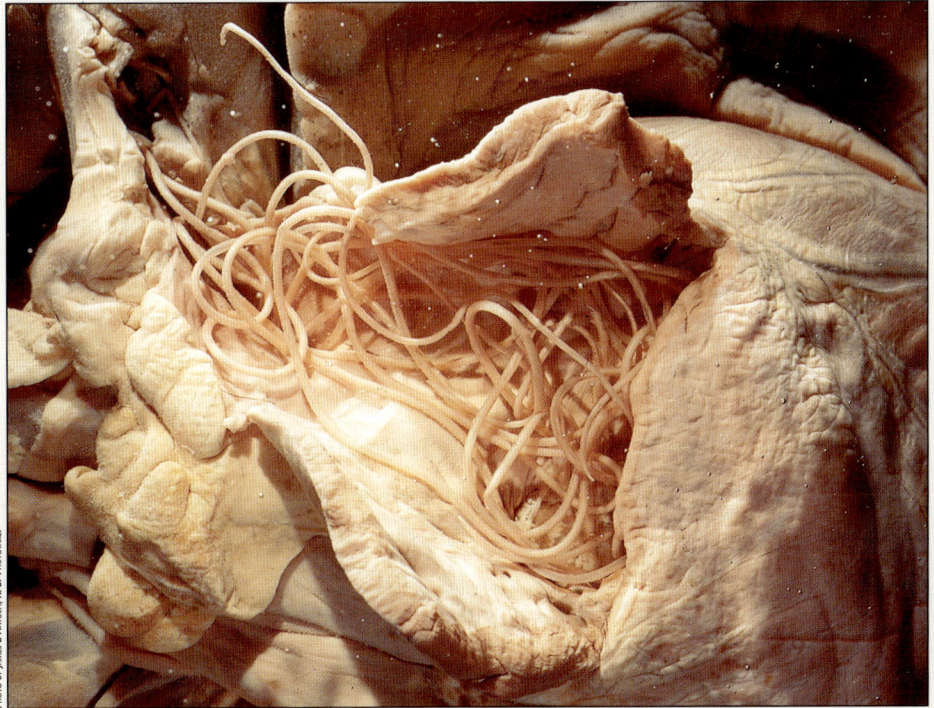

The heart of a dog infected with canine heartworm, *Dirofilaria immitis.*

HOMEOPATHY:
an alternative to conventional medicine

CURING OUR DOGS NATURALLY

Holistic medicine means treating the whole animal as a unique, perfect living being. Generally, holistic treatments do not suppress the symptoms that the body naturally produces, as do most medications prescribed by conventional doctors and vets. Holistic methods seek to cure disease by regaining balance and harmony in the patient's environment. Some of these methods include use of nutritional therapy, herbs, flower essences, aromatherapy, acupuncture, massage, chiropractic and, of course, the most popular holistic approach, homeopathy.

Homeopathy is a theory or system of treating illness with small doses of substances which, if administered in larger quantities, would produce the symptoms that the patient already has. This approach is often described as 'like cures like.' Although modern veterinary medicine is geared toward the 'quick fix,' homeopathy relies on the belief that, given the time, the body is able to heal itself and return to its natural, healthy state.

Choosing a remedy to cure a problem in our dogs is the difficult part of homeopathy. Consult with your veterinary surgeon for a professional diagnosis of your dog's symptoms. Often these symptoms

'Less is Most'

Using this principle, the strength of an homeopathic remedy is measured by the number of serial dilutions that were undertaken to create it. The greater the number of serial dilutions, the greater the strength of the homeopathic remedy. The potency of a remedy that has been made by making a dilution of 1 part in 100 parts (or 1/100) is 1c or 1cH. If this remedy is subjected to a series of further dilutions, each one being 1/100, a more dilute and stronger remedy is produced. If the remedy is diluted in this way six times, it is called 6c or 6cH. A dilution of 6c is 1 part in 1,000,000,000,000. In general, higher potencies in more frequent doses are better for acute symptoms and lower potencies in more infrequent doses are more useful for chronic, long-standing problems.

Health Care

require immediate conventional care. If your vet is willing, and knowledgeable, you may attempt an homeopathic remedy. Be aware that cortisone prevents homeopathic remedies from working. There are hundreds of possibilities and combinations to cure many problems in dogs, from basic physical problems such as excessive moulting, fleas or other parasites, unattractive doggy odour, bad breath, upset tummy, obesity, dry, oily or dull coat, diarrhoea, ear problems or eye discharge (including tears and dry or mucousy matter), to behavioural abnormalities such as fear of loud noises, habitual licking, poor appetite, excessive barking and various phobias. From alumina to zincum metallicum, the remedies span the planet and the imagination…from flowers and weeds to chemicals, insect droppings, diesel smoke and volcanic ash.

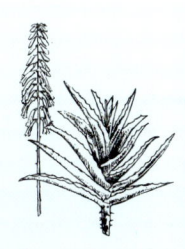

Using 'Like to Treat Like'

Unlike conventional medicines that suppress symptoms, homeopathic remedies treat illnesses with small doses of substances that, if administered in larger quantities, would produce the symptoms that the patient already has. While the same homeopathic remedy can be used to treat different symptoms in different dogs, here are some interesting remedies and their uses.

Apis Mellifica
(made from honey bee venom) can be used for allergies or to reduce swelling that occurs in acutely infected kidneys.

Diesel Smoke
can be used to help control travel sickness.

Calcarea Fluorica
(made from calcium fluoride, which helps harden bone structure) can be useful in treating hard lumps in tissues.

Natrum Muriaticum
(made from common salt, sodium chloride) is useful in treating thin, thirsty dogs.

Nitricum Acidum
(made from nitric acid) is used for symptoms you would expect to see from contact with acids, such as lesions, especially where the skin joins the linings of body orifices or openings such as the lips and nostrils.

Symphytum
(made from the herb Knitbone, *Symphytum officianale*) is used to encourage bones to heal.

Urtica Urens
(made from the common stinging nettle) is used in treating painful, irritating rashes.

Number-One Killer Disease in Dogs: CANCER

In every age, there is a word associated with a disease or plague that causes humans to shudder. In the 21st century, that word is 'cancer.' Just as cancer is the leading cause of death in humans, it claims nearly half the lives of dogs that die from a natural disease as well as half the dogs that die over the age of ten years.

Described as a genetic disease, cancer becomes a greater risk as the dog ages. Veterinary surgeons and dog owners have become increasingly aware of the threat of cancer to dogs. Statistics reveal that one dog in every five will develop cancer, the most common of which is skin cancer. Many cancers, including prostate, ovarian and breast cancer, can be avoided by spaying and neutering our dogs by the age of six months.

Early detection of cancer can save or extend your dog's life, so it is absolutely vital for owners to have their dogs examined by a qualified veterinary surgeon or oncologist immediately upon detection of any abnormality. Certain dietary guidelines have also proven to reduce the onset and spread of cancer. Foods based on fish rather than beef, due to the presence of Omega-3 fatty acids, are recommended. Other amino acids such as glutamine have significant benefits for canines, particularly those breeds that show a greater susceptibility to cancer.

Cancer management and treatments promise hope for future generations of canines. Since the disease is genetic, breeders should never breed a dog whose parents, grandparents and any related siblings have developed cancer. It is difficult to know whether to exclude an otherwise healthy dog from a breeding programme as the disease does not manifest itself until the dog's senior years.

RECOGNISE CANCER WARNING SIGNS

Since early detection can possibly rescue your dog from becoming a cancer statistic, it is essential for owners to recognise the possible signs and seek the assistance of a qualified professional.

- Abnormal bumps or lumps that continue to grow
- Bleeding or discharge from any body cavity
- Persistent stiffness or lameness
- Recurrent sores or sores that do not heal
- Inappetence
- Breathing difficulties
- Weight loss
- Bad breath or odours
- General malaise and fatigue
- Eating and swallowing problems
- Difficulty urinating and defecating

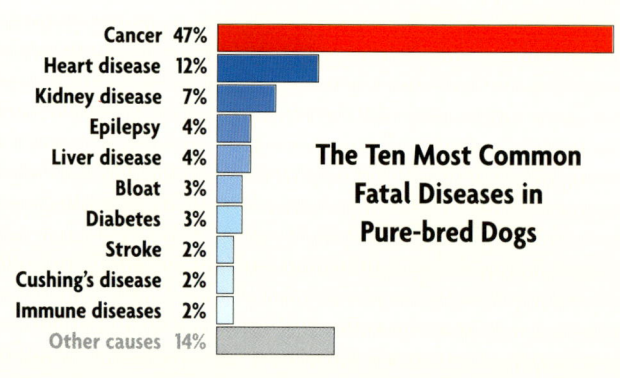

The Ten Most Common Fatal Diseases in Pure-bred Dogs

Disease	Percentage
Cancer	47%
Heart disease	12%
Kidney disease	7%
Epilepsy	4%
Liver disease	4%
Bloat	3%
Diabetes	3%
Stroke	2%
Cushing's disease	2%
Immune diseases	2%
Other causes	14%

Recognising a Sick Dog

Unlike colicky babies and cranky children, our canine charges cannot tell us when they are feeling ill. Therefore, there are a number of signs that owners can identify to know that their dogs are not feeling well.

Take note for physical manifestations such as:

- unusual, bad odour, including bad breath
- excessive moulting
- wax in the ears, chronic ear irritation
- oily, flaky, dull haircoat
- mucous, tearing or similar discharge in the eyes
- fleas or mites
- mucous in stool, diarrhoea
- sensitivity to petting or handling
- licking at paws, scratching face, etc.

Keep an eye out for behavioural changes as well including:

- lethargy, idleness
- lack of patience or general irritability
- lack of interest in food
- phobias (fear of people, loud noises, etc.)
- strange behaviour, suspicion, fear
- coprophagia
- more frequent barking
- whimpering, crying

Get Well Soon

You don't need a DVR or a BVMA to provide good TLC to your sick or recovering dog, but you do need to pay attention to some details that normally wouldn't bother him. The following tips will aid Fido's recovery and get him back on his paws again:

- Keep his space free of irritating smells, like heavy perfumes and air fresheners.
- Rest is the best medicine! Avoid harsh lighting that will prevent your dog from sleeping. Shade him from bright sunlight during the day and dim the lights in the evening.
- Keep the noise level down. Animals are more sensitive to sound when they are sick.
- Be attentive to any necessary temperature adjustments. A dog with a fever needs a cool room and cold liquids. A bitch that is whelping or recovering from surgery will be more comfortable in a warm room, consuming warm liquids and food.
- You wouldn't send a sick child back to school early, so don't rush your dog back into a full routine until he seems absolutely ready.

INDEX

Page numbers in **boldface** indicate illustrations.

A series (Agouti) 48
Aarnipuro line 18
Aarnipuro, Jakke 18
Abilities 35
Activity 120, 125
—level 87
Adult
—diet 87
—health 134
—training 101
Affection 33
Age 105
Ageing 134
Aggression 83
—fear 119
Agility trials 36, 89, 123
Air travel 98
AKC 27, 29
AKC Foundation Stock
  Service 27
Allergy
—airborne 135
—food 136
American dog tick 142, **143**
American Kennel Club 27
American Rare Breed
  Association 27
Anal region 95
Ancylostoma caninum **147**
Andrews, Zena Thorn 25
Appetite 87
ARBA 27
Arthritis 136
Ascaris lumbricoides **146**
Athleticism 35
Attention 111
Australia 31
Auto-immune illness 135
Axelrod, Dr Herbert R 145
B (Brown) series 48
Balai directive 22
Barking 38
Bedding 72, 81, 85, 106
Bite 40, 67
Blaster 92
Blood tracking 123
Boarding 98
Body 43
Bones 74, 95, 134
Booster immunisations 133
Boredom 36
Borrelia burgdorferi **143**
Bowls 76
Brambleway Kennels 30
Brandes, Miss Sarah 25
Breed club 125
Breed standard 56
—approval of 17
—differences among 57
—first 9

Breeder 56
—selecting a 63
Breeding age 64
Broome 17
Brown dog tick 145
Brushing 90, 92
Burkwalls 28
C (Colour) series 48
Cail, Norma 36
Cancer 154
Canine development
  schedule 105
Car travel 97
Carlacot kennel 22
Carlsen, Mr Georg 25
Cat 110
Cat-like characteristics 37,
  42
Cataracts 19, 34
Cats 38
Chelville kennels 21
Chetwynd, J and P 21
Chew toys 73, 84
Chewing 78, 107
Cheyletiellosis 144
Chiggers 145
Children 38, 83
Coat 15, 18, 35, 54, 65, 93
Coat length 15, 66
Coat maintenance 89
Code of ethics 63
Collar 74, 111
Colour 10, 13, 26, 45, 48, 65-
  66
—genetics of 47
Combing 90
Come 115
Commands 103, 112, 117
Control 106
Coronavirus 133
Crate 70, 72, 85, 97-98, 104,
  106
—training 72, 102, 106, 109
Crose, Gae 27-28
Crying 81, 85
Ctenocephalides canis **138**
Curdeleon kennel 21
De Buffon, Georges Louis
  10
Deer tick 143
Demodex 144
Denmark 22, 31
Dental care 94, 134
Dental health 137
Dermacentor variabilis **142-
  143**
Dermanyssus gallinae 145
Destructive behaviours 36,
  73, 107
Dewclaws 44

Diet 86, 136
—adult 87
—junior 87
—puppy 86
—sheet 87
—veteran 134
Digging 38, 79
Dipylidium caninum 148
Dirofilaria immitis **151**
Discipline 107, 109
Distemper 133
Documents 68
Dog flea 138
Dog tick 143
Dogs for the disabled 36
Dominance 83
Down 113
Down/stay 114
Druse, Madelin 27-28
Dunger, Roger and Sue 20
E (Extension) series 50
Ears 41
—care 95
—mite 145
Echinococcus multilocularis
  148
Elbereth kennels 20
Elkhound 50
Eronen, Kylikki 30
Eskimo dogs 11
Eutrombicula alfreddugesi
  145
Exercise 37, 88-89
—puppy 89
External parasites 138-145
Eyes 40
—care 95
—defects 33
Family dog 9, 38
Family introduction to pup 80
Faults 55
FCI 27, 45, 48
Fear period 82
Fédération Cynologique
  Internationale 27
Feeding 86, 136
—amounts 87
—schedule 88
Feet 44, 91
Fence 79
Finland 33, 36
—breed register 15
Finnish Kennel Association
  11, 13
Finnish Kennel Club 11, 14-15,
  19, 34, 56
Finnish Lapphund breed club
  63
Finnish Lapphund Club 19
—of Great Britain 22, 34

Finnish Spitz 11
Finnish Spitz Organisation 13
First aid 132
Flea 138-142, 148
—life cycle 139-141
Food 86, 136
—allergies 136
—amounts 87
—intolerance 137
—rewards 111-113, 118
—storage 86
Forequarters 43
France 31
Friendly nature 38
FSS 27, 29
Gait 53
Garden 79
Gender differences 65
Generalised progressive
  retinal atrophy 33
Genetics of colour 47
Glenchess kennel 22
Gottorp kennel 26
Gottorp, Mrs Margit 26
GPRA 33
Graungaard, Mrs Kirsten 25
Grooming 89, 93
—equipment 90
Guard dog 35
Guarding 9
HC 19, 63
Head 38
Health 33
—concerns 33
—dental 137
—testing 19, 63
Hearing dogs for the deaf
  36
Heartworm 149-**151**
—life cycle **148**
—prevention 149
Heel 116
Height 55
Hepatitis 133
Herding dogs 11, 15, 36
Herding instincts 9, 38
Hereditary cataracts 19, 26,
  34, 63
Hereditary conditions 33
Hereditary skin disorders
  135
Hildrek kennel 22
Hindquarters 44
Hip dysplasia 19, 26, 64
Holistic medicine 152
Holland 29, 31
Home preparation for pup
  69
Homeopathy 152-153
—remedy 153

Hookworm **147**
—larva **147**
House-training 70, 102, 109
—timetable 103, 108
Housing 104
Hunting instinct 9
Identification 99
IGR 140, 142
Importation of dogs 20, 27
Inari kennel 25
Independence 36-37
Insect Growth Regulator 140, 142
Insurance 129
Intelligence 32, 35-36
Internal parasites 145-151
Jackson, Toni 20
Judges 56
Juhls 17
Junior diet 87
Karelian Bear Dogs 11
Keeshond 50
Kennel Club, The 22, 34, 45, 68
Kennel cough 133
Kennel Lumipyri 30
Kennel Sarky Feny 30
Kennel v.d. Nieuwenkamp 30
Koira kennel 24, 26
Kremsreiter, Sharon 28
Kukonharjulainen 11
Kukonharjun 11
Kuusisto, Jukka 20
Lapinkoira 17
Lapinporokoira 15, 18
Lapland 10
Lappalaiskoiratry 18-19
Lapphund Club of Finland 18
Lappish Herder 11
Lappish Kennel District 13
Lapponian Herder 11, 15, 17-18
Lead 74, 111
Lecibsin kennel 15, 20
Lehtinen, Hans 25
Leptospirosis 133
Lice 144
Life expectancy 33
Livestock 38
Lupus 136
Lyme disease 90
Mange mite 144
Marden, Linda 27-28
Maturity 64, 87, 89
Mite 143
Moulting 54, 91
Mouth 40
Movement 53
Musta vaalein merkein 48
Muzzelle, Mr and Mrs C 21
Muzzle 38
Nail trimming 97

National dogs of Finland 32
Natural dogs 15
Neck 42
Negative reinforcement 110
Neutering 134
Nipping 84
Nisula, Mr Rauno 121
Norway 31
Nose 38, 50
Obedience classes 100, 102, 119
Obedience competition 119
Obedience trials 36, 120
Obesity 87
Olenov 11
Origins 32
—of breed 9
Osteoarthritis 136
Otodectes cynotis 145
Ownership 67
Paimenkoira 11
Paimensukuinen Lapinkoira 18
Paimensukuinen Lapinkoiran Seura 19
Paimensukuinen lines 19, 44-45
Paimensukuinen linja 48
Paimensukuinen type 63
Paimensukuisen Lapinkoiran Seura 19
Paimensukuisen linja 24
Parainfluenza 133
Parasite
—bites 135
—external 138-145
—internal 145-151
Parkki 48
Parvovirus 133
PAT work 37, 120-121
Pedigree 64
Pennardane kennel 22
People-oriented 32
Peski kennel 15, 24
Pet Passport Scheme 22
Pets as therapy 120-121
PEVISA health schemes 33
PEVISA system 19
Physical characteristics 38
Pigmentation 50
Pollen allergies 135
Popularity 35
Poromiehen kennel 15
Positive reinforcement 102, 110
Poultry mite 145
PRA 19, 21, 26, 35, 63
Praise 102, 111-113, 118
Preventative medicine 129
Pricked ears 41
Progressive retinal atrophy 19, 63
Psoroptes bovis 144

Punishment 107, 110
Puppy
—appearance 63
—diet 86-87
—exercise 89
—first night home 80
—health 131
—problems 82, 84-85
—selection 63-65
—temperament 67
—training 101
Puppy-proofing 77, 79
Pystykorva 11
Rabies 133
Reindeer dog 10
Reindeer farming 9-10
—advances in 11, 15
Rewards 110-113, 118
Rhabditis **146**
Rhipicephalus sanguineus **145**
Roundworm **146**
Ruotsinlapinkoira 18
Saame farmers 10, 15, 33
Safety 70, 78, 107
—harness 98
Sarcoptes 144
SCANDIA 30
Search and rescue 36, 122
Seare, Ros and Col 31
Separation anxiety 85
Separation of breeds 14-15
Show potential 66
Showing classes 119
Sit 112
Sit/stay 114
Size 35
—early 11
Skin problems 134
—inherited 135
Snow-nose 50
Socialisation 36, 65, 82-83
Society for the Original Reindeer Herder 19
Spaying 134
Spectacles 50, **51**
Spitz 11
—breeds 9, 50
Standard 56
Stay 114
Strongyloides 149
Sugarok kennel 27-28
Sulyka Kennels 20, 30
Suomenlapinkoira 17
Sweden 31
Swedish Lapphund 18
Switzerland 31
Tail 52
Takanen, Matti 22, 26
Tapeworm 148
Teeth 40, 67, 73, 84, 94, 129, 134
Temperament 32, 35, 38
—evaluation 131

Temperature 32, 38
Theldaroy kennels 31
Thorndike's Theory of Learning 110
Thorndike, Dr Edward 110
Threadworm 149
Tick 90, **142-143**
Tipped ears 41
Toilet training 102, 109
Topcoat 90
Toxocara canis 146
Toys 73, 85, 95, 106
Tracheobronchitis 133
Tracking 36, 122
Trainability 35-36, 121
Training 83
—consistency 114
—crate 106
—equipment 111
Travelling 70
—air 98
—car 97
Treats 111-113, 118
Trichuris vulpis 148
Type 63
—working vs. show 18
UK 15
—importations into 20
Undercoat 90
US
—imports into 27
Uthaug, Turid 22, 25
Vaccinations 80, 82-83, 131
Vainio, Marri 15, 24
Variable ratio reward system 118
Versatility 36
Vet 79, 134, 145
—insurance 129
—selecting a 127
—specialist 127, 135
Veteran diet 134
Von Duben, Professor Gustaf 11
Von Linne, Carl 10
Walking dandruff 144
War years 11
Watchdog 35
Water 88, 106
Weaning 129
Weather 32
Weight 55
Whining 81, 85
Whipworm 148-149
With other dogs 38
Wolverine 35
Working ability 32
Working lines 18, 24
Working tests 36
Working trials 36, 89, 124
X-register 15
Y-register 14

My Finnish Lapphund

PUT YOUR PUPPY'S FIRST PICTURE HERE

Dog's Name _____

Date _____ Photographer _____